ROLLING STOCKS

MAKING
MONEY
ON THE
UPS
AND
DOWNS

New Strategies for Cash Flow
and Wealth Enhancement

ROLLING STOCKS

MAKING

MONEY

ON THE

UPS

AND

DOWNS

GREGORY WITT

With Foreword By
Wade B. Cook

Lighthouse Publishing Group, Inc.
Seattle, Washington

Lighthouse Publishing Group, Inc.
Copyright © 1998, 1999 by Gregory Witt

Library of Congress Cataloging-in-Publication Data
Witt, Gregory
Rolling Stocks; Making money on the ups and downs/
Gregory Witt; with foreword by Wade B. Cook
p. cm.
1. Stocks. 2. Speculation. 3. Rollovers (Finance) 4. Cash flow.
I. Title.
HG6041.W58   1998
332.63'228--dc21   98-10271
ISBN (cloth) 0-910019-63-0

"This publication is designed to provide accurate and authoritative information in regard to the subject matter covered. It is sold with the understanding that the publisher is not engaged in rendering legal, accounting, or other professional service. If legal or other expert assistance is required, the services of a competent professional person should be sought."

From a declaration of principles jointly adopted by a
committee of the American Bar Association and the committee
of the Publisher's Association.

Balance of Power™, Time Segmented Volume™, Cumulative MoneyStream™, and Telechart 2000© are the exclusive intellectual property of Worden Brothers, Inc. The descriptions, examples, and analysis of these have been used with their permission. For further information contact Worden Brothers, Inc., 5 Oaks Office Park, 4905 Pine Cone Drive, Durham, North Carolina 27707, 1-800-776-4940.

Book Design by Judy Burkhalter
Dust Jacket by Angela Wilson and Cynthia Fliege
Production: Brent Magarrell

Published by Lighthouse Publishing Group, Inc.
14675 Interurban Avenue South
Seattle, WA 98168-4664
1-800-706-8657
206-901-3100 (fax)
Source Code: RS99R2

Printed in the United States of America
First Edition 1998
Second Edition 1999
10 9 8 7 6 5 4 3 2 1

TO:
MOM AND DAD

ACKNOWLEDGMENTS

If you want to find out what it feels like to be overwhelmed by a task, write a book. The deeper you get into the project, the more you come to value the talents and resources of countless friends, family members, and professionals in many areas of expertise.

I offer my sincere appreciation to the staff of Lighthouse Publishing for their technical and editorial expertise. A special thanks goes to Alison Curtis and Cheryle Hamilton who have nurtured this book from its inception.

To the many talented people at Wade Cook Seminars who have been involved in developing and teaching many of the strategies encompassed in this book, I give my highest professional accolades. They are a constant stream of encouragement, ideas, and inspiration. Wade Cook, John Childers, and Joel Black have been generous with their time and powerful in their influence.

And to my wife, Elain, and to my family, I give my love for their patience, sacrifice, and continual support.

CONTENTS

INDEX I

INDEX II

INDEX III

FOREWORD

BY WADE B. COOK

Author of *Wall Street Money Machine, Stock Market Miracles, Business Buy The Bible,* and *Bear Market Baloney*

It is such a pleasure to see one of my basic strategies in the stock market (one for generating tons of cash flow) take on new and dynamic dimensions. Greg Witt has added new insights to this remarkable way of making money.

Rolling Stocks should have been the first book I wrote. Why? Because it takes my first and most fundamental strategy, Rolling Stocks, and covers it in depth. *Rolling Stocks* will teach you how to make phenomenal returns using the same strategy that started me on my incredible rendezvous with wealth in the stock market.

Rolling Stocks gives you all the tools and techniques you need to generate cash flow and accumulate wealth using just this one strategy. Filled with examples and easy-to-follow formulas, it will enable you to uncover the patterns and secrets of this powerful technique.

The author, Gregory Witt, is a seasoned, professional investor, and a member of Team Wall Street. He has brought together years of experience, combined with exhaustive research into *Rolling Stocks*. The result is a fast-paced, thorough, guided tour of how you can make big returns with Rolling Stocks.

Great books have always been an important part of my life. I grew up feeding my mind great ideas by reading books about success. *Rolling Stocks* is that kind of book. As you read *Rolling Stocks*, imagine yourself doing each of the steps outlined. Mentally put yourself in the frame of mind to make investments that will put you on the fast track to becoming financially independent.

Once you have positioned yourself *mentally* for financial success, then the proven strategies, formulas, and patterns that are revealed in this book will make it a *reality*. Don't settle for anything less.

Wade B Cook

PREFACE

I remember my introduction to the principles taught by Wade Cook. A friend visiting in my home told me that he was reading *Wall Street Money Machine* and bragged about the returns he was getting. I had been an investor for many years and was naturally curious to find out what Wade Cook had to offer that could achieve the kinds of results I was after.

"What's Wade Cook's strategy?" I asked.

"Buy low, sell high," was my friend's response.

We both chuckled at his surprisingly simple summary. But I got the feeling that Wade Cook was offering something substantially different than was being offered elsewhere. So I enrolled in the Wall Street Workshop™ for myself and learned that Wade Cook's successful strategies and formulas go far beyond that elementary evaluation. But at their core is the basic notion of selling stock for a profit and doing it *repeatedly* in a disciplined manner.

Rolling Stocks is Wade Cook's first and most fundamental strategy, yet as investors become more knowledgeable and experienced in the stock market, they often turn most of their attention to more sophisticated strategies involving options. They get excited, and justifiably so, about greater rewards. But they also take on a greater risk. Don't get me wrong, I love options. I make my living in the stock market. I am a full time investor. I spend much of my day studying, evaluating and trading stock options. But that's not where I place the bulk of my portfolio. Like most investors, I want the majority of my investments to be in assets that don't require constant attention but still give me a predictable return.

With that goal in mind, I set out to become an expert in one strategy. I wanted to learn everything I could possibly know about Rolling Stocks. I wanted to do my homework and learn every possible angle. More importantly, I wanted to prove my knowledge in the trenches of the market. I committed to an aggressive program of practicing what I knew about Rolling Stocks. The results continue to amaze me. The returns keep coming in and the strategy keeps on working for me.

In September, 1997, Wade invited me to conduct a roundtable discussion on Rolling Stock strategies at Winstock '97 in Las Vegas. It was a wonderful opportunity to meet in small groups with graduates of his Wall Street Workshop™. These people were serious investors, most of whom had some good experience under their belt in stock market investing. Most of them were trading options and were profitable at it. Yet they came to the workshop recognizing that when it came to consistently using the Rolling Stock strategy on a long-term basis, they needed to be refreshed.

Sure, they had tried trading some Rolling Stocks. Many of them had used the strategy on a repeated basis for several months. But when the stocks they were trading stopped rolling, they went on to other investments. To keep the strategy working for them, they needed to have their skills updated and uncover stocks that were currently rolling. Once they gained these skills, they left full of enthusiasm about their ability to make money with the Rolling Stock strategy again.

I wrote this book as a means of sharing my experience and expertise with a wider audience. I wanted to share the secrets of how to make the strategy work for anyone. It really can work for anyone, but just knowing about the Rolling Stock strategy is not enough. You need to learn the basic rules and equip yourself with the formulas and methods to make it happen. My intent has been to include everything you need to make the strategy work for you.

It would be easy to fill a book with illustrations of stocks that are rolling, but that would be a giant disservice to the reader. Not only would the information be outdated before the book was published, but the reader would still lack the knowledge of how to find and manage a portfolio of Rolling Stocks. Therefore, the examples and case studies supplied in the book are done so to teach specific aspects of the Rolling Stock strategy.

There is a well-known proverb that says: "Give a man a fish and he'll eat for a day. Teach a man to fish and he'll eat for a lifetime." I want to teach you everything you need to know to fish for Rolling Stocks. I'm not talking about a hobby. I'm talking about some serious commercial fishing!

Most people will spend their entire life trying to acquire wealth. Most will achieve little more than paying the bills only to retire dependent on the government or whatever savings they have been able to put away. I find that to be a sad situation.

Our educational institutions have done a poor job of teaching young people how to acquire wealth. Just try to find textbooks or handbooks on generating cash flow or becoming financially independent in public libraries or in the mass media. Wealth education has never been found in America's colleges and universities. That kind of specific, yet essential, knowledge isn't found easily.

I recently visited some of the largest public libraries and university libraries in the United States. I was looking for books that gave solid, hands-on strategies and tools for the average investor. I went away empty handed. I went to the business school library at America's largest private university. They had only one book on investing in the stock market and no book that dealt with options trading for the typical investor.

I realized there was a crying need for this wealth-building education. Americans are investing in the stock market more than ever before. There are over 50 million brokerage accounts open in the United States. Over 130 million people are investing indirectly through mutual funds. I firmly believe that many of those who invest in mutual funds do so not because they expect to outperform the stock market (they generally have not over the past few years), but because they lack the requisite knowledge to jump into the market and invest directly.

As you come to understand the Rolling Stock strategy you will also come to understand basic concepts and techniques used by successful investors. You will become familiar with tools for the technical and fundamental analysis of stocks. Your confidence and skill as a trader will be developed into a highly disciplined art.

The strategies and techniques in this book will enable you to be one of those who has the knowledge and confidence to invest directly and successfully. You will know how to uncover your own Rolling Stocks. But that's only the first step. You'll be able to plan your entrance and exit for a consistently profitable return. You'll know which stocks to avoid and how to protect yourself against losses. You'll learn power strategies that can boost your returns significantly. You'll learn how to adapt your Rolling Stock strategy to options for even greater potential returns.

Now it's time to roll up our sleeves and go to work. Making money in the stock market won't happen until you are armed with the knowledge to make it happen. Once you have the knowledge, then a dedicated, disciplined approach will give you the kinds of results you're after. Read on.

1

THE FUNDAMENTALS

FIRST, A DEFINITION

The term "Rolling Stock" was coined by Wade Cook, one of America's premier financial strategists. It's one of those coined terms that has caught on quickly among investors. That's probably because it's easy to understand and because it conveys a mental picture of a stock chart with a rolling, wavelike pattern.

Rolling Stock can be defined as a stock which fluctuates between support and resistance. Let's expand on that concept a bit: Rolling Stock is the stock of any company whose price fluctuates (or rolls) between a low range or "floor" (commonly referred to as support) and a high range or "ceiling" (commonly referred to as resistance). Support and resistance are familiar terms in the stock market and have been used for years by market analysts to identify the price range within which a stock trades.

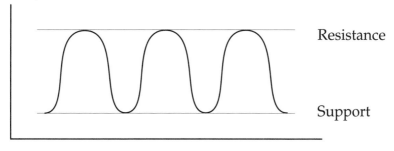

Resistance

Support

"Risk varies inversely with knowledge."

—IRVING FULLER

If you were to look up the term Rolling Stock in any dictionary you would find something completely different from what we are talking about here. Webster, for example, defines Rolling Stock as "the wheeled vehicles of a railroad, including locomotives, freight cars, and passenger cars." That definition had its origins in the 1850s when the expanding railroad was the pulse of our nation's emerging economy. But today, the pulse of the American economy, even the world economy, is the stock market. So perhaps it's fitting to have a new definition for today's economy.

The notion that some stocks tend to fluctuate in a predictable pattern between support and resistance is not new. The concept of "channeling" has long been used by stock market technicians to describe stocks that roll between support and resistance. But it was Wade Cook who gave wings to this concept and turned it into the cash flow tool that has made record returns for the individual investors who apply his strategies.

WHERE IT ALL BEGAN

The origins of Wade Cook's experience with Rolling Stocks goes back to his early days as an investor. Here is his story in his own words:

"I got a call one day from a stockbroker. He said 'Wade, I know how disappointed you are with your stock market investments. But I want to take you to lunch.' At lunch that day, he said 'I want you to buy some Motorola stock at $50 a share.' So I did. I bought 100 shares (That's $5,000 plus about $80 in

---

"If principles can become dated, they're not principles."
—WARREN BUFFETT

commissions). He said, 'Now, put in an order to sell this stock when it gets to $60.'

Sure enough, about six or seven weeks later this stock climbed up to $60. I ended up selling it. I sold it for $6,000 and had about $90 in commissions. So all in all, I made an $830 profit.

Then he said, 'Now, I want you to buy it again at $50 a share.' So, I put in the order to buy it when it got down to $50. And sure enough, a little over a month later it was back down to $50 and I bought another 100 shares.

Then he said, 'Put in an order to sell at $60.' I said, 'How do you know it's going to go back up to $60?' He said, 'Wade, I've been doing this for three years. Just put in the order.' So I put in the order at $60 and sure enough, it went back up to $60. I sold it and made just under $1,000 again.

One time when I sold it at $60, it went up to $62 and I said, 'Oh man, I missed out on some of the profits.' And one time when I bought it at $50 the stock went down to $49 and to $48, and I was getting kind of worried about it. But it went right back up to $60.

I did this with Motorola for 3¹/₂ years! I call this 'Rolling Stock.' I found my first way to use the stock market as a cash flow machine."

"Men of genius do not excel in a profession because they labor in it; they labor in it because they excel."

—WILLIAM HAZLITT

Out of this initial experience the Rolling Stock strategy has been developed and refined. It has been taught to thousands and used successfully by investors at all levels of experience. Those investors who take a longer term "buy and hold" approach can use Rolling Stock to diversify, generate greater cash flow, and profit from the rolling pattern of selected stocks even when the broader market is trending down.

This strategy can also work successfully for more aggressive traders. Traders typically have a more short-term approach to the market. Rolling Stock fits well with that approach and trading style, since most of the Rolling Stocks are only held for a period of no more than two or three months.

As an investor, I use a number of different strategies. I have long term investments in blue chip stocks, I invest in some stocks for their dividend income, I generate cash from some stocks by writing covered calls, and I also trade in options. But I've always viewed the Rolling Stock strategy as the *most important* strategy I use.

Why is it so important for any investor to understand Rolling Stock? It is because your understanding and ability with Rolling Stock will impact and carry over to every other stock market strategy. Once you've mastered the techniques covered in this book you'll not only be proficient at making money in Rolling Stocks, but you'll find that your knowledge will transfer easily to the options market. Learning the Rolling Stock strategy and becoming a disciplined trader in this strategy will also help you understand the broader market.

"Greed is a bottomless pit which exhausts the person in an endless effort to satisfy the need without ever reaching satisfaction."
—ERICH FROMM

What if you're an experienced trader who has been trading options with less than spectacular results? Can this book still help you? By all means. It can help you identify the patterns and movements common to all stocks. It can improve your timing as a buyer and help you limit losses and maximize profits as a seller. You'll be surprised at the impact it has on your options trading. Pay particular attention to the patterns and strategies discussed in Chapter 10 on Rolling Options.

I like to compare what I do to a basketball coach. Ask any coach what the most important skill in basketball is. I've never seen a coach spend hours training his players how to make three-point shots or slam-dunks. Most great coaches drill the basics such as ball handling, dribbling, and passing.

I believe that to keep your Rolling Stock skills well tuned and working, you need to use them daily. Every portfolio should include some Rolling Stocks which can be rotated in and out. Blue chip stocks and other growth stocks should form the foundation of your portfolio. You may also choose to invest a portion of your account in the options market. Rolling Stock is an aggressive strategy that should be a highly profitable part of any portfolio.

As I teach the Rolling Stock strategy in seminars across the country, I still get excited watching students come alive with learning as they hear about the strategy for the first time. The excitement intensifies as they watch the deals being done in class. Then the focus shifts from me, the facilitator to the par-

"If I had known then what I know now, I would have made the same mistakes sooner."

—ROBERT HALF

ticipants themselves as they begin to actually do these trades in class while on the phone with their brokers.

Many of these students will approach me weeks or months later saying something like this, "Hey, remember those 1,000 shares of XYZ company I bought during the workshop? (We've done so many successful deals, I admit I sometimes don't remember.) Well, I've rolled the stock three times since then for a 20% profit each time!" As a teacher, that is my greatest reward.

I have found that those who make the most money over the long haul are those who learn the Rolling Stock strategy, and then practice it diligently and repeatedly. They often make mistakes in the process and generally learn more from their mistakes than they do from their successes.

I have even seen students who keep a journal describing their trades and evaluate their results using the gift of hindsight. They report that when they take the time to evaluate how and why they made or lost money some clear patterns emerge. They make money when they follow the rules and apply the formulas consistently. On those occasions when they lose money, they can nearly always pinpoint a breakdown or flaw in the application of the strategy. To put it bluntly, they broke the rules.

So what are the rules of Rolling Stock? What is it you need to know? More importantly, *what is it you need to do* consistently to make money on your trades and avoid losses? Let's begin with the fundamentals.

"There is no security on this earth. There is only opportunity."
—Douglas MacArthur

There are three rules which I believe are guiding principles for success in Rolling Stocks. Throughout the remaining chapters I will uncover specific strategies, practices, and procedures to apply at specific points in the trade. I will share with you the results of years of research into Rolling Stocks—where to find them, what makes them move, when to get in, and when to get out—but I will never depart from these key rules, only build on them.

RULE #1 - KNOW WHEN TO GET OUT

You need to know when and where to exit before you ever get in. I've never known a firefighter that didn't live by this rule. Getting *into* a burning building is easy. But everything changes once inside. The clear air, oxygen level, lack of obstructions, and the ability to see and hear clearly are often gone once inside a burning building. The firefighter's life depends on knowing that the exit may not be the same door he used as an entrance.

As a successful investor in Rolling Stocks, you need to have an exit strategy in place on both the upside and the downside. You need to be able to express that strategy to yourself and to your broker if necessary, before you enter the trade. You should understand what that exit point means in both actual dollars and in a percentage rate of return.

In most cases, that exit point, or the price at which you sell your Rolling Stock will be when the stock reaches the resistance line. That point will be covered later. But there will also

"I have made a fortune by selling too soon."

—J. P. MORGAN

be situations where you will want to adjust your exit either up or down as circumstances change.

If a stock is moving up and performing well, you may decide to cancel a sell order and hold the stock as it moves up beyond its resistance level. Or, if a stock has gone up, but appears to be losing momentum, you may choose to sell early as a means of locking in your profits and putting your money in another investment with better profit potential.

By establishing your exit, you've made it clear that the reason you bought the stock was to sell it for a profit. You don't make that profit until you sell the stock. Remember that Rolling Stocks are bought with the expectation that they will go back down again. Therefore, your immediate objective will always be to sell the stock before it goes back down.

I've actually heard people suggest that it isn't useful to predetermine a downside exit strategy prior to placing a trade. They claim that this kind of negative thinking is detrimental to their potential success in the market. I disagree. A stock doesn't know you own it, and your positive attitude will be powerless in stopping a stock in a downward trend.

An exit strategy on the downside exists to insure you against losses that could conceivably outweigh any upside potential. A reporter once asked a football coach with a lifelong record of winning how he had achieved that feat. The answer was simple: "Don't lose." By predetermining your stop-loss or downside exit point, you prevent losses, which could prove

---

"Luck is what happens when preparation meets opportunity."
—DARREL ROYAL

catastrophic. This strategy will help to keep you in the overall winning position in spite of an occasional loss.

We'll cover the process of determining when to get in and when to get out in greater detail in Chapters 5 and 6. Right now just know that the surest way to establish your exit is to use a two-step order process. The first step is to place the order to purchase the stock. The second step, which can be made as you buy the stock or immediately thereafter, is to place a Good 'Till Canceled (GTC) order to sell your stock. It costs you nothing to place this sell order. You can change it at any point in the future by simply calling your broker and requesting the change. But having that exit point established tells both you and your broker that you have an overall plan of attack and expectation for your account.

RULE #2 - DON'T BE GREEDY

There is an old Wall Street maxim: *Bulls get fed, and bears get fed, but hogs get slaughtered.* In the workings of the market, greed will do more harm than good to your bottom line.

As Wade Cook pointed out in his experience with Motorola, there were times when he failed to sell at the peak and buy at the lowest point. Many profitable traders are content to capture just 50 to 75% of a stock's roll. Sure, there may be others who hope to capture 90 to 100% of a roll, but by operating in a more narrow range, you'll come out a bigger winner in the long run.

"It takes twenty years to make an overnight success."
—EDDIE CANTOR

When you try to buy at the absolute bottom of a roll, your likelihood of being taken for a downside ride increases. Before I buy, I prefer to see a stock start to reverse its downward trend and show some signs of upward movement.

When you get greedy on the top end, you may be able to squeeze an additional profit out of the position, but it may take you an extra couple of weeks or more for just one or two additional percentage points. In the same time you could have moved on to another position and already made your next profit.

For now, please put aside profit/loss analysis. For just a moment don't even consider what the financial return may or may not be from a particular entrance or exit point. Look at it from a more philosophical frame of mind. Let me ask you: is there enough profit to be gained in the stock market to completely satisfy all your needs and wants? Of course there is!

The stock market is not a zero-sum game. It's not a winner-take-all proposition. There is so much abundance and earning potential in the stock market that it simply doesn't make sense to let your trading decisions be driven by an emotion such as greed. It can very quickly become counterproductive. And believe me, you'll enjoy the stock market and life in general a lot more by learning to put greed behind you.

RULE #3 - FOCUS ON INEXPENSIVE STOCKS

Why inexpensive, lower priced stocks? And just what constitutes a lower priced stock? I'm not going to become too clini-

---

"God gave me my money."

—JOHN D. ROCKEFELLER

cal here. And I'm not going to say that you should never roll a stock over $20 or $30. The point is to do just as the rule says: focus on lower priced stocks.

Let's compare it to driving a car. You *focus* on the road ahead of you. All the while your field of vision is constantly taking in a much wider view. You occasionally shift your focus to read a billboard or to look at the person in the passenger seat. But you quickly return your focus to the road ahead of you. Similarly, your focus will be on lower priced stocks.

My experience and research show that lower priced stocks (typically those under $20) will not only give you *more rolls* over the course of a year, but will give you a *higher percentage rate of return on each roll*. Additionally, you will find that once they stop rolling, they tend to go up, rather than down, thereby providing you a little more protection on the exit.

Lower priced stocks enable you to parcel out your risk in bite-sized chunks. Instead of buying 100 shares of a $75 stock for $7,500 you can buy 1,000 shares of a $2 stock for just $2,000. For many small investors, this may be the most they want to put at risk.

Using this same example, you can diversify much more easily by using lower priced stocks. For the $7,500 you would have spent on 100 shares of the higher priced stock, you can now buy 1,000 shares each of two or three different stocks in the $2 to $3 range.

"Money is like an arm or a leg. Use it or lose it."
—HENRY FORD

Lower priced stocks also give you greater flexibility in terms of building your share purchases each time you roll. What do I mean by that? Here's an example:

Let's say you have $5,000 to invest and you want to reinvest your profits so that your principle will continue to grow. You decide to invest in a Rolling Stock and you purchase 100 shares at $50 per share. When the stock goes to $60 you sell your shares for $6,000. When it comes time to purchase more shares at $50 you will probably end up buying an odd lot of 120 shares. Not impossible, but sometimes less profitable.

Stocks generally trade in round lots, or blocks of 100 shares. Odd lots (trades not in 100 share increments) generally trade at a premium of $1/8$ to $1/4$ of a point. Odd lots also slow the trading process, especially for stocks which do not trade on major exchanges. For example, if you placed your order for 120 shares, it would trade in two transactions, one for 100 shares, and another for 20 shares. This odd lot transaction for 120 shares will often cost you more in commissions than a comparable transaction for only 100 shares.

Using the same example, let's take that same $5,000 and put it into 1,000 shares of a $5 stock. If you sell at $6 your proceeds are still $6,000. When it comes time to buy back in at $5, you are able to buy a round lot of 1,200 shares. This is typically a more liquid transaction and can often result in a lower commission.

"Experience is a hard teacher because she gives the test first, the lesson afterwards."

—VERNON LAW

With these fundamentals in place, we're ready to move on to the more detailed specifics of Rolling Stocks. These detailed strategies will help you make your Rolling Stocks all the more profitable and put your portfolio on track to help you reach your financial dreams.

"Success consists in the climb."

—ELBERT HUBBARD

2
ROLLING TO RICHES

If you are like most investors you probably started out in the stock market by buying a stock with the intent of holding on to it for a long time. As you gained experience and confidence in your investing ability, you realized that by buying on dips and selling on strength, you could generate greater returns.

The Rolling Stock strategy takes that basic principle and multiplies it repeatedly. By focusing on repeated, short-term gains, there is a cumulative and compounded return that you won't find with a "buy and hold" strategy. The Rolling Stock strategy increases the emphasis on the selling of stock. The fact is, if you are like most investors, you don't spend a lot of time thinking about selling stock.

If you are like most investors I talk with, you will be able to quickly understand and apply the Rolling Stock strategy. In fact, I've never taught this strategy and then had someone say "I don't get it," or "Please explain that again; I didn't understand what you were doing." Rolling Stock is such a simple, powerful strategy that it's never misunderstood.

My challenge is to help investors recognize how really effective a Rolling Stock strategy can be in generating cash quickly and in transforming a small account into a large account in a short time frame.

"The greatest accomplishment is not in never falling, but in rising again after you fall."

—VINCE LOMBARDI

Fortunately there are plenty of great examples to illustrate the power of Rolling Stocks. If you doubt the effectiveness of Rolling Stocks or if you think there just isn't enough to be gained by buying on dips, let's see what we can learn from this example.

JUST AN EXAMPLE

To demonstrate the power of Rolling Stocks, let me show you a straightforward, real life example of the kind of phenomenal returns Rolling Stocks can generate. The name of the company we'll use for our example is Just Toys Inc. (Ticker JUST).

For illustrative purposes, I am not going to mention commissions in this example. Commissions are a real cost of trading, as are capital gains taxes. You should never fail to take the cost of commissions into account as you determine your entrance and exit point. I'll talk about managing commissions in Chapters 6 and 11, but let's learn the fundamental strategy first.

In this example I am going to put all numbers in dollars and cents rather than fractions. This will make it easier to follow and relate our holdings to our real life pocketbook. Thus, $2^{13}/_{32}$ becomes \$2.41. Not only does it make sense to more people, but it also represents the current trend, as several markets have chosen to convert to decimals in 1998.

Just Toys Inc. designs, develops, manufactures, and markets toys, sports equipment, and games. Their stock trades on the NASDAQ under the ticker JUST. They make AirZone sports toys and polyvinyl chloride bendable figures

---

"If you think you can, you can. If you think you can't, you're right."
—MARY KAY ASH

known as Bend-Ems. Most of these toys are based on characters from Disney, Warner, and 20th Century Fox cartoons. The company sells to mass merchandisers such as Wal-Mart, KMart, Target, and Toys R Us.

The stock traded as high as $23 in 1993 and made a steady decline through most of 1994 on disappointing earnings. By 1995 the stock was trading in a more stable pattern under $3 a share. As you can see this is no Intel; it's not even a Mattel!

To make spectacular returns in Rolling Stocks you don't need to find a high-flying growth company. Let's take a look at how a repeated roll can turn a small fortune into a much larger fortune in a short period of time.

Roll #1. During May and early June, 1995, Just Toys (JUST) established support at $1.25 per share. It traded as low as $1, but it would have been easy on any of several days to buy it at $1.25 or less. For the sake of this example, let's be conservative and say that you purchased 1,000 shares for $1.25 or a total investment of $1,250.

At this point, the first rule of Rolling Stock comes into play: "Know when to get out." That is, determine where and when you will sell. By looking at the chart, we can determine that the previous support level of $2 would be a likely new resistance level. So we then put in a Good Till Canceled (GTC) order to sell at $2.

"Nine-tenths of wisdom consists in being wise in time."
—THEODORE ROOSEVELT

Within three weeks the stock was trading around $2 per share. It even went as high as $2.44 on one day, and traded for several days at $2.25 or higher. Now the second rule comes into play: "Don't be greedy." We don't have to catch the absolute top and bottom of the range to make phenomenal returns. All the technical indicators were saying "sell, sell, sell." Some of these technical indicators include volume, stochastics, moving averages and other factors. Our GTC did its job and we were filled at $2. Our initial investment of $1,250 has now grown to $2,000 in just a few short weeks.

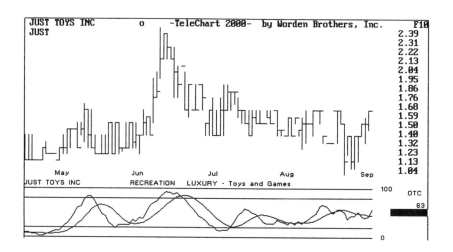

	Buy	Price of Stock	Shares	Cost	Price of Stock	Sell	Proceeds
Roll 1	6-95	$1.25	1,000	$1,250	$2	6-95	$2,000

"All progress has resulted from people who take unpopular positions."

—ADLAI STEVENSON

Roll #2. By late August, JUST was trading back in the $1.25 range. It traded in this range for a full week. During that time you could have bought for as low as $1. Let's stay on the conservative side and put our buy order in for $1.25

In no less than four days the price of the stock shot up to our exit price of $2 per share. If your GTC was in place your stock would have sold. Over the next month the stock traded around and above the $2 range. It even went as high as $2.63 in both September and October.

Roll #3. By December, JUST had slowly declined back down to a decent buy range. You could have bought it at or below $1.25 for over a week. But the best technical indicators had us buying it on December 27th.

Patience is a good virtue to have in the stock market, because you had to wait 49 trading days before the stock hit $2. Again, you would have been filled on February 28, 1996 at $2 but only if your had your GTC in place.

Roll #4. It took only 19 trading days in March for JUST to slide back down to the $1.25 buy range. The stock drops as low as $1.13, but we wait for the optimal technical buy signals and purchased it at $1.25. Needless to say, we put in a GTC to sell at $2

Thank goodness the GTC was in place. Within two days the stock jumped to $2 and we got out. We then move on to other opportunities while the stock moves down to our buy range.

"Success is never final."

—WINSTON CHURCHILL

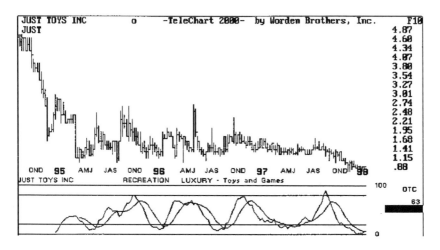

	Buy	Price of Stock	Shares	Cost	Price of Stock	Sell	Proceeds
Roll 1	6-95	$1.25	1,000	$1,250	$2	6-95	$2,000
Roll 2	8-95	$1.25	1,600	$2,000	$2	8-95	$3,200
Roll 3	12-95	$1.25	2,560	$3,200	$2	2-96	$5,120
Roll 4	4-96	$1.25	4,096	$5,120	$2	4-96	$8,192

Roll #5. This buying opportunity occurs in just 17 trading days as we saw the stock go as low as $1. But again, let's be conservative and make our entrance at $1.25 on April 29, 1996. We put in our GTC then hold our shares and wait 24 trading days and watch our stock be sold for $2 a share on June 3rd.

Roll #6. Greed tempts us and we almost start to kick ourselves as the stock goes up to a high of $2.69. But that sour grapes feeling is short lived as JUST makes its predictable slide back down to the $1.25 range in 18 days.

"We know what a person thinks not when he tells us what he thinks, but by his actions."

—ISAAC BASHEVIS SINGER

During August, 1996, the stock traded at or below $1.25 for three weeks. During this time the stock goes as low as $1.06. We watch the technical indicators and buy at the end of the trough at $1.25.

We make our smooth entrance and put in our GTC to sell at $2 a share. Within 14 trading days the stock hits $2 and we are out on August 5, 1996. This time its retreat is more precipitous and falls back to the buy range in just seven days.

Roll #7. JUST stays in the $1.25 buy range for over a month. The technical indicators are particularly weak. We could get in at any time for $1.25, but if we wait for the strongest signals, we buy back in on September 17th.

In just 24 trading days our prized possession made its familiar climb back up to $2. Our GTC to sell is doing its job and we are filled on October 21st.

Following the seventh roll and the sale of the stock, JUST flattened out in a narrower range. It stayed in that range for over a year. Finally, in November, 1997, JUST fell down into the $1.25 range. The technical indicators were particularly weak, and I saw no compelling buy opportunity.

The stock continued to fall below the $1 level at the time of this writing. Technical indicators remain weak, but I continue to monitor both the fundamentals of the company and the technical indicators on the stock price.

"I had no ambition to make a fortune. Mere money-making has never been my god. I had an ambition to build."

—JOHN D. ROCKEFELLER

As you can see, by applying the Rolling Stocks strategy and using the techniques which detail in the following chapters you could have rolled JUST seven times in 17 months. But the most exciting part is what happened to your trading capital in each successive roll.

Assuming you reinvested your initial trading capital and continued using the proceeds of each sale to buy more shares, your initial investment of $1,250 to buy 1,000 shares would have grown to 16,777 shares which would have generated cash proceeds in your account of $33,553. That's a 2,584% rate of return in just 17 months!

	Buy	Price of Stock	Shares	Cost	Price of Stock	Sell	Proceeds
Roll 1	6-95	$1.25	1,000	$1,250	$2	6-95	$2,000
Roll 2	8-95	$1.25	1,600	$2,000	$2	8-95	$3,200
Roll 3	12-95	$1.25	2,560	$3,200	$2	2-96	$5,120
Roll 4	4-96	$1.25	4,096	$5,120	$2	4-96	$8,192
Roll 5	4-96	$1.25	6,553	$8,192	$2	6-96	$13,107
Roll 6	7-96	$1.25	10,485	$13,107	$2	8-96	$20,971
Roll 7	9-96	$1.25	16,777	$20,971	$2	10-96	$33,553

Also, in the above example, your money wasn't even invested most of the time. While you were waiting for JUST to make its descent back to the $1.25 buy range, you could have taken the proceeds and invested those in another Rolling Stock.

Maybe it's not realistic to expect that the average investor could have caught all seven rolls. But even if you caught only four or five of the rolls, you would have walked away with a

---

"Try not to become a man of success but rather a man of value."
—ALBERT EINSTEIN

555% rate of return in less than a year. Is that better than what you're currently getting?

Now you decide. Are you ready to learn the Rolling Stock strategy? Are you ready to turn your stock market account into a cash flow locomotive? Do these kinds of returns on publicly traded companies interest you? Then let's keep rolling!

"You can't steal second base and keep one foot on first."
—ANONYMOUS

3

TIPS: HOT AND COLD

This chapter is about advice, both good and bad. In the stock market, knowing where *not* to get advice can be more valuable than knowing where to get it. No investor operates in a vacuum. I've never met an investor that gathers data in a world devoid of emotion and then acts on that data without input from any outside source. Nearly everyone seeks input from multiple sources and balances that input with their own analysis and sentiments.

Is it easy to find Rolling Stocks? Using traditional means, it's harder than you might think. I've never had a broker call me up and say, "Here's a great little Rolling Stock for you to buy." Most stockbrokers don't actively track and play inexpensive Rolling Stocks. When Rolling Stocks do appear, brokers aren't likely to get too excited about them.

Brokers typically recommend stocks that are widely held and heavily traded. They know and follow those stocks which other analysts, particularly those in their own firm, are following and rating. Brokers are more interested in a stock ready to make its big move from $30 to $40 than a stock that moves between $3 and $4 repeatedly.

"If two people agree all the time, one of them is unnecessary."
—DAVID MAHONEY

Even when you call a broker with a potential Rolling Stock, don't be surprised or disappointed if he doesn't share your enthusiasm for the stock and its potential. You may look at a chart and see a great Rolling Stock. They may look at the same chart and see a lackluster stock trading at the same price it was at three years ago.

This difference in perspective is important. If your perspective is "buy and hold," then Rolling Stocks make no sense at all. If, however, you buy stocks so that you can sell them, knowing that you only make money when you sell, then Rolling Stocks should make your heart beat a little faster.

Again, don't be disappointed or intimidated if your broker doesn't share your interest in a potential Rolling Stock. It may take several months of repeated success before they see the method of your strategy.

It should be easy to find Rolling Stocks on your own, right? After all, don't all stocks go up and down? Yes, all stocks fluctuate, but that doesn't make every stock a Rolling Stock. In fact, I have found that less than 2% of all stocks can be characterized as Rolling Stocks during the course of a year.

ROLLING STOCKS - WHAT QUALIFIES

Perhaps my standard is more stringent than most, but I consider a stock to be a Rolling Stock if it offers at least three buying opportunities at a particular price which will each yield a 15% rate of return during a twelve month period. Because I'm not overly concerned about buying at the abso-

---

"With enough insider information and a million dollars, you can go broke in a year."

—WARREN BUFFETT

lute bottom and selling at the absolute top, I may not be able to realize the full 15% return on each trade. But even if I were only to capture 10% on three rolls in a year, that would be a 33% compounded annualized return. By setting this as my *minimal* standard I have chosen a rate of return which would outperform the broader market.

The Rolling Stock Standard:
Three or more buying opportunities in a 12 month period at a specific price, each of which will yield at least a 15% rate of return.

Let me give you a simple visual example: as you can see from the illustration, there were at least three points at which you could have purchased this stock at $3 per share and subsequently sold it at $4 per share. Yes, there were times when the stock went above $4. There were also times when you might

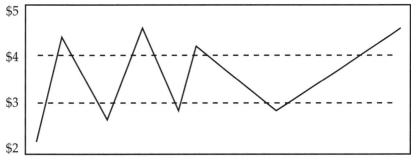

| | Jan | Feb | Mar | Apr | May | Jun | Jul | Aug | Sep | Oct | Nov | Dec |

"When you lose in the stock market, don't blame the bulls and the bears, but the bum steers."

—Market Maxim

have purchased the stock at $3 only to watch it decline to a lower level. But it quickly bounced off of that floor only to work its way back to a ceiling of $4 or greater.

This illustration should be helpful not only in defining what a Rolling Stock is, but in showing you that the easiest way to spot a Rolling Stock is by looking at a chart. I have looked at hundreds of charts with one eye closed and a pencil held horizontally against the chart. This simple, lo-tech method is about as effective as the most expensive charting technology on the market when it comes to visually spotting Rolling Stocks.

I am so tuned in to Rolling Stocks that I can't look at a stock chart without immediately asking myself, "Is this a Rolling Stock?" I've even been known to look at an EKG and think "Wouldn't this make a great Rolling Stock?" I make my living in the stock market and generally scan a minimum of 100 charts a day. In the process, I make a log of Rolling Stocks and find that I'm constantly adding to that list.

But frankly, most investors getting started in Rolling Stocks want a reliable tool for uncovering Rolling Stocks without having to get an advanced degree in statistics or becoming an expert in technical analysis of stocks. So let's look at those resources that will identify Rolling Stocks for you.

WEALTH INFORMATION NETWORK™ (W.I.N.™)

W.I.N.™ is a subscription online service that provides a wide variety of investment information. It has a section on Rolling Stocks and includes updates during trading hours of stocks

---

"When we ask for advice, we are usually looking for an accomplice."
—MARQUIS DE LA GRANGE

that are actively rolling and which appear to be in a buy range. W.I.N.™ also includes regular reports from Wade Cook and his trading department.

A more detailed explanation of W.I.N.™ is included in Appendix I showing sample entries and subscription information.

Other Online Sites

The Internet has changed the way most of us gather and retrieve information. Nowhere has this change had more impact than on the stock market. With millions of us now able to make stock and option trades online, there has been an information explosion which has been a great benefit to the individual investor.

With this information also comes risk. On the Internet everyone is now a worldwide publisher. Issues of accountability and credibility are tested. It is important to caution investors that not everyone with a website is worthy of emulation. Free advice can often turn out to be very expensive. I admit to learning this the hard way when it comes to the stock market. The school of hard knocks gives a great education, but the tuition can be costly.

I have received countless solicitations from services, some free and some offered on a subscription basis. These services typically originate as an e-mail solicitation. They promise to feature a "stock of the month" or a "hot stock tip." They typically tell you how their last stock pick resulted in some phenomenal return.

"If stock market experts were so expert, they would be buying stocks, not selling advice."

—Norman Augustine

Be advised that many of these services are paid sales and public relations agents of the company they are touting. Provided they meet certain SEC guidelines and disclose their financial relationship with the company they are recommending, they are within their rights to make these recommendations. If you want to find this required disclaimer on their literature, I can save you a lot of time by suggesting you start at the end of the recommendation and look for the small print.

Certainly, some of these recommendations have resulted in potentially profitable situations. However, usually by the time the stock is recommended to you, the smart money has made its move, the efficient market has responded, and you can easily wind up a day late and many dollars short.

The market maxim says to buy on rumor and sell on fact. I sometimes wonder whether rumor is any basis for a buying decision. I'm reminded of a joke about gold traders which applies nicely to stock traders:

A trader dies and goes to heaven. He meets St. Peter and tells him of all his wonderful traits. St. Peter admits that the trader deserves to be in heaven. There's just one problem: there isn't room for another trader. The trader was disappointed and asked if he could at least see the place where the other traders reside in heaven.

St. Peter agrees and leads him to a room where traders sit around in beautiful surroundings, being pampered, and living the good life. The trader begged St. Peter: "Isn't there *any* way

---

"The trouble with advice is that you can't tell if it's good or bad until you've taken it."

—FRANK TYGER

to get in?" Saint Peter says that the only way would be for someone to give up his spot and reside in hell.

Thinking quickly, the trader opened the door to the room and shouted, "There's been a huge gold discovery in hell!" Immediately the traders poured out of the room and headed for hell.

Suddenly, the trader who started the rumor left St. Peter's side and began running with the crowd. St. Peter yelled "Hey! Where are *you* going?" The trader yelled back, "You never know, there might be some truth to the rumor!"

Rumors feed the herd, and on Wall Street, the herd mentality is what we want to avoid. You'll be safer and richer when you stay apart from the herd mentality.

I have also had my fill of anything labeled "insider information." Even if the information you have is legally obtained, it is implausible that the market hasn't already acted in some way on this information. This is true of the stock market and even more true of the options market.

For these reasons I generally recommend, especially for the less experienced investor, that you carefully consider the source of your advice. Is there a hidden agenda? Are they trying to sell you a particular stock or investment?

Determine the actual track record of the person giving the advice. Perhaps the simplest test of all is this: is the person I'm listening to making the kind of money I want to make? There is

---

"Committees seem to be as poor in selecting stock as in composing sonnets."

—Murphy Teigh Bloom

some safety and a certain amount of peace of mind that comes from arming yourself with the appropriate knowledge, using sound strategies, and gathering data from reliable sources.

CHARTING SOFTWARE

I find most of my Rolling Stocks while scanning stock charts. For those of us who make our living in the stock market, chasing down these stocks is half the fun. My strategy for uncovering Rolling Stocks is to use professional charting software to which I apply my own sorting parameters. After I've scanned thousands of stocks, I sort out those that meet certain technical criteria. I then look for stochastic data that has proven to be predictive for that stock over the past year.

If the term "stochastic data" or "stochastics" is unfamiliar to you, don't worry, that won't keep you from making money in the stock market. I've found that many of the industry insiders who hear and use the term have only a vague idea of what it really means.

Stochastics come from the Greek word *stochastes* meaning "diviner." Stochastics are a statistical tool used by market technicians in determining whether a stock's price is overbought or oversold. In the stock market, stochastics use a stock's historic trading range and price movement as a basis for indicating the direction of the stock's future movement. A charting service, which provides stochastic analysis, is a powerful tool for identifying the right buying and selling

"Many of life's failures are people who did not realize how close they were to success when they gave up."
—THOMAS EDISON

opportunity. I have included the stochastics lines on the stock charts in this book. They appear in the lower third of the chart below the price graph.

There are a number of Internet-based stock charting services that allow you to enter a stock name or ticker symbol and bring up a current price and graph showing the stock's movement over the past year. These services are helpful if you know the company you're looking for. What they lack is the ability to search the thousands of listed stocks by means of user-driven parameters.

In order to efficiently search and scan stocks using my own specifications, I use TeleChart 2000©. This is a professional stock charting service. It provides historic charts for nearly 10,000 stocks. It allows you to customize the chart and to display the information you find most useful. You can update the charts every night by a toll-free modem access. You can then run a variety of scans using the criteria you choose. I have found charting software to be the least expensive professional tool available to the average investor.

Let's say, for example, you want to find all stocks under $5 per share, with volume above a certain level and with stochastics that showed potential for upward movement. You would be able to enter these parameters, run the scan, and in a matter of minutes have a manageable list of maybe 100 stocks which you could scan instead of the thousands of available stocks.

"It's what you learn after you know it all that counts."
—JOHN WOODEN

Once you've visually identified potential Rolling Stocks, TeleChart 2000© includes tools for determining the stock's historic support and resistance. From the chart you can also determine the length of the roll, the average percentage gain, and the average rate of return.

In addition to this historical market data, TeleChart 2000© features several proprietary indicators. These are tools of technical analysis such as Balance of Power™, MoneyStream™, and Time Segmented Volume™. These tools chart price trends, stock volume and hidden patterns of buying and selling which can assist in predicting the movement of the stock.

Most charting software also allows you to create "watchlists," or selected groups of stocks you can monitor on an ongoing basis. For example, I have created a list of nearly 100 stocks under $5 that have been rolling in the past year. I also have a similar list of Rolling Stocks in the $5 to $10 range. I have several other watchlists for other types of stocks I want to follow.

Charting software also enables you to scan thousands of stocks by computer using customized criteria. For example, you can quickly scan for all stocks which have had five consecutive advancing days, or have just crossed below their 40 day moving average, or have had a percentage decline of over 10% in the last trading session.

Armed with these resources you will have an abundant supply of Rolling Stock candidates from which to choose. You

"The illiterate of the future will not be the person who cannot read. It will be the person who does not know how to learn."
—ALVIN TOFFLER

may find that with a list of only 10 or more Rolling Stocks you will have enough potential investment opportunities to get you off to a great start.

"There is only one success—to be able to spend your life in your own way."

—Christopher Morley

4
WHERE THEY HIDE

PATTERNS FOR PROFIT

My friend Rich loves to fish. He spends many of his weekends and entire weeks during the summer, fishing. He knows more about fishing and how to catch fish than most of us will ever know. He has a collection of rods, lures, and flies that are worth more than some people's stock portfolios.

One day I was preparing to take my son on a trip to the lake that would include some fishing. I wanted to make it a great father-son experience but I knew that meant actually catching some fish. I realized I had almost no fishing experience, so I asked Rich what his secret was for finding fish, great fish, lots of fish.

"No secret," he said. "You just fish where the fish *are*, and don't waste your time fishing where they *aren't*."

Rich spends enough time fishing that he literally knows where the fish are. He knows the time of day when certain fish are likely to bite. He knows the depth at which they swim. He knows the parts of the lake or stream where they are most likely to be.

"Money is like manure. If you spread it around, it does a lot of good, but if you pile it up in one place, it stinks like hell."
—CLINT W. MURCHISON

That same kind of experience, knowledge, and intuitive radar can lead you to find Rolling Stocks. I've made it my specialty to learn where Rolling Stocks hide, when to buy them, and when to avoid them. This research and experience will make your investing more profitable and it will also keep you out of trouble by helping you to recognize situations which could lead to losses.

Some people are able to make decisions about buying or selling stocks during trading hours in a matter of seconds. I find my best plays are born before or after trading hours in the quiet of my office as I pore over technical charts and fundamental analysis. There is no right or wrong way to trade here, just a matter of personal style and preference.

So when it came to getting a firm grasp on Rolling Stocks, I decided to put to the test many of the market rules and much of the conventional wisdom. I launched an exhaustive research effort into Rolling Stocks. I analyzed the charts of thousands of companies. I wanted to quantify relationships between Rolling Stocks and trading volume, earnings, and stock price. I looked at technical factors such as Balance of Power™, MoneyStream™, and stochastics, to see how they might predict a roll.

I then developed a set of hypotheses which I could test. I admit these hypotheses were not developed from a purely objective and scientific method frame of mind. My own trading experience had already led me to trust and act on many of these hypotheses. But I wanted to prove to myself that there was reason and rationality in what I was doing. As a

"The market, like the Lord, helps those who help themselves."
—WARREN BUFFETT

result, what I am sharing in this chapter is the distillation of years of trading experience further proven by quantitative research on thousands of stocks.

I have already seen my success in trading Rolling Stocks increase as I have acted on these hypotheses. With each profitable trade I come to rely on them even more as tested and proven strategies. They have become rules of conduct for my Rolling Stock trades. These have become the patterns I look for so I can drop my line where the fish are, and not waste my time fishing where they aren't.

HYPOTHESIS #1: ROLLING STOCKS ARE MORE COMMONLY FOUND IN THE LOWER PRICE RANGES

In studying the charts of thousands of companies, I found good Rolling Stocks at a variety of price levels. But I found more Rolling Stocks, *many more Rolling Stocks*, at the lower price levels. As I sorted stocks into groups based on their price range (Under $5, $5 to $10, $10 to $20, $20 to $30, $30 to $40, $40 to $50 and over $50) I found a greater concentration of Rolling Stocks *every time* I lowered the price range.

In fact, if you are looking for Rolling Stocks, the one place *not* to look is in the higher price ranges. I only found one stock that rolled during the past year in a price range above $80. That stock was Intel (INTC) prior to its 2:1 split. There was just one other, Wells Fargo (WFC), that came close. It traded three times in the $255 to $285 price range, but never quite yielded a 15% rate of return on each roll. Remember, I

"Success is more a function of consistent common sense than it is of genius."

—AN WANG

look for stocks that have offered three buying opportunities at the same price, each of which yielded at least a 15% rate of return over the course of a year.

As I continued doing research in the higher priced stocks (stocks over $50), I found only ten stocks that had met my definition of a Rolling Stock. In each case, these stocks met only the minimal requirements. Each of them had rolled only three times. If you exclude the beating most stocks took on October 27, 1997, when the Dow dropped 550 points, the number of Rolling Stocks over $50 goes from ten to just five.

The main reason that higher priced stocks are less likely to roll is because most investors tend to think in terms of dollar movements rather than in percentages. A $5 stock that goes to $6 never gets much attention. But when a $70 goes up to $80, investors get excited. In actuality, the rate of return (percentage increase) is greater for the $5 stock.

Not surprisingly, as we move down into stocks in the $5 to $10 range, the number of active Rolling Stocks increases dramatically. When we drop below $5 the number of Rolling Stocks goes up again.

The message here is this: if you want to find Rolling Stocks, you need to hang out where the Rolling Stocks hang out. You need to do your looking in the lower price ranges. If you want to see Rolling Stocks pay out quickly and profitably, you need to do most of your fishing in the streams marked "$10 and under."

"To win you have to risk loss."

—JEAN-CLAUDE KILLY

There are plenty of great blue-chip companies in the $30 and over price range that I love to trade and hold in my portfolio. I would never discourage you from buying those stocks given the right circumstances. But when it comes to generating cash flow from small, repetitive Rolling Stocks, keep your focus on lower priced stocks.

HYPOTHESIS #2: LOWER PRICED STOCKS TEND TO ROLL FASTER

One thing to keep in mind is that you buy stocks so that you can sell stocks. You make money in the stock market as you convert cash to assets (stocks) and back to cash. The faster you can profitably move cash to assets and back to cash, the more money you make.

So as I look for Rolling Stocks, I want to find those opportunities that have the potential of achieving my targeted return as quickly as possible. No one would argue that stocks are risky. So why would a person want to put their cash at risk for three months if they could achieve the same rate of return by putting their cash at risk for one month or less?

When I went looking for stocks that rolled quickly, I looked for stocks that had the shortest duration between the buy-in point and the sell point. I'm not as concerned about having to wait for the stock to go back down to a buy-in price. That's why I don't measure a roll from one buy-in point to the next buy-in point. My focus is "how fast can I sell this stock?" So I measure the duration of the roll from bottom to top.

"God will not look you over for medals, degrees, or diplomas, but for scars."

—ELBERT HUBBARD

I look for those opportunities where the duration of the roll can be measured in days. If I can be in and out in less than a month, I'm happy. If I can be in and out in a week or less, I'm ecstatic!

Those quick in-and-out opportunities are consistently more abundant in lower priced stocks. Again, the lower the price, the quicker the roll. In lower priced Rolling Stocks, it's not uncommon to see a stock whose trading range on a given day may equate to 10% of the stock's price.

Celtrix Pharmaceutical (CTRX) had eight rolls of over 15% during 1997. With a minor adjustment in your buy-in point, you could have caught all of these rolls quite easily. Even if you had set a firm buy-in point of $2^1/_8$ and a sell point of $2^1/_2$ you would have missed the highest peaks and lowest valleys, but you would have still caught five of those rolls for a return of 17% on each roll.

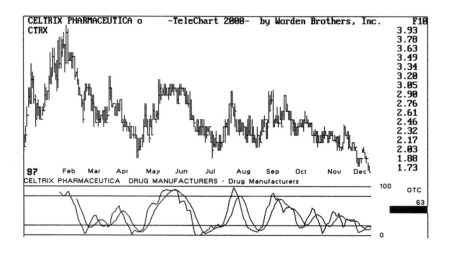

"Some people wait so long for their ship to come in, their pier collapses."

—JOHN GODDARD

Notice that when the stock is on the upswing, the duration of the roll is generally two weeks or less. However, when the stock is trending downward, the time it takes to get back down to its buy-in point is longer. I like this pattern in a Rolling Stock. This enables me to get in, make my return quickly, and get out. I don't mind having to be patient for the stock to go down.

A closer look at the chart reveals that on many days the stock's trading range can move the stock up 10 to 15%. On some of the larger peaks, the stock moves up to 20% of its share price in one day. Once your GTC is in place, this kind of volatility can work in your favor.

HYPOTHESIS #3: LOWER PRICED STOCKS HAVE GREATER PERCENTAGE INCREASES

When a high-priced stock goes from $100 to $110 there is $10 worth of profit potential. When a lower priced stock goes from $2 to $3 there is just a $1 increase, but a far greater profit potential in terms of the percentage increase. Because the actual dollar movement is much smaller, the movement tends to be less noticed by the market. Most investors understand that rationale, but I still felt it was important to test this hypothesis.

My research verified that lower priced Rolling Stocks move up more quickly, but as I suggested in the previous example of CTRX, they make larger percentage advances in each day's trading.

"I like to buy stocks when the bears are giving them away."
—WARREN BUFFETT

The following chart provides a good illustration of how a low-priced stock can move the full range of the roll in a day's trading.

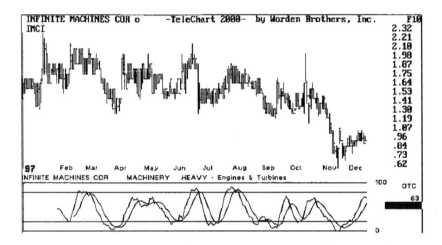

Infinite Machines Corp. (IMCI) is another example of a stock whose price consistently makes large percentage moves. Since it trades under $2 per share, it nearly always moves a full 10% daily. Daily moves of 20 or 30% are not uncommon. This provides an excellent opportunity for those who have their GTC ready and waiting for both the buy and the sell.

HYPOTHESIS #4: ROLLING STOCKS TEND TO EMERGE AFTER A STOCK HAS FALLEN FROM A HIGHER PRICE LEVEL

A stock that is rolling wasn't always rolling. It had to come from somewhere, right? If you want to find Rolling Stocks early, doesn't it make sense to find where they come from so that you're more likely to catch them as they start to roll?

"Necessity is the mother of taking chances."

—MARK TWAIN

The great majority of all Rolling Stocks settle into a rolling pattern as a result of a decline from a higher trading range. In fact, over 85% of Rolling Stocks in the $10 and under range traded higher in the six months preceding the rolling pattern. This is a powerful signal to help you spot an emerging roller.

The typical pattern is one in which a stock may have been overvalued due to great earnings expectations or perhaps even unwarranted hype. The price of the stock goes up to an overbought or overvalued level. Eventually something happens which takes the air out of the balloon. The stock price moves downward and the stock becomes more accurately valued. As the company continues on a more stable path, the price of the stock goes into a roll until some significant fundamental factor jolts it out of its roll.

The five-year chart of Orthologic (OLGC) displays this common pattern in Rolling Stocks. A stock that trades in a range

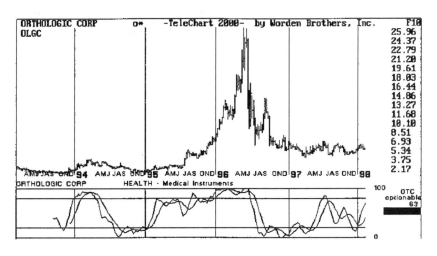

"People who take risks are the people you'll lose against."
—JOHN SCULLEY

of $1 to $3 makes a bold move upward, often on expectation of a new product or major inroads into the marketplace.

In this case, the stock went up to over $20 per share. As those expectations fail to materialize or as setbacks occur, the stock retreats to its previously established trading level.

This pattern provides you as the investor with some level of insurance. The fact that a stock has traded at a higher level often suggests that the "fluff," "hype," and "air" has been taken out of the stock's price, so that you have a more reasonably priced stock. This can usually be verified as you do your home-work and check into the company's long term stability and growth history.

Some people think that because a stock has fallen dramati-cally, it can't go any lower. Wrong! The old adage "don't catch a falling knife" works well here. Don't buy something just be-cause it's low-priced. Make sure the fundamentals and techni-cal analysis suggest solid upside potential. Make sure it has started rolling up before you buy.

HYPOTHESIS #5: ROLLING STOCKS TEND TO GO UP AFTER THEY FINISH ROLLING

Since Rolling Stocks don't roll forever, where do they go after they are done rolling? If the tendency were for them to "fall off the earth" or go down to zero, that would be a fright-ening prospect. Every time you purchased in at the bottom of the roll, there would be a likely possibility that your invest-ment would head south.

"You can measure opportunity by the same yardstick that measures the risk involved. They go together."

—EARL NIGHTINGALE

Of course, that possibility always exists, but in most Rolling Stocks the odds are against it happening. My research seems to show that after a stock has completed its rolling pattern, it tends to move up to a higher trading range. Occasionally the stock will "flatten out," or go sideways, but more frequently the trend is upward.

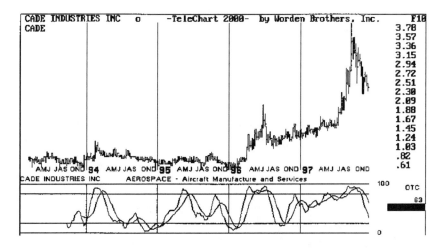

The chart for Cade Industries (CADE) shows how a stock can roll predictably for several years in a given range (in this example, 50¢ to $1). Finally, the stock takes off and breaks out of its roll. In this case, the risk is the lost opportunity. But that is far more attractive than the risk of losing the value of your assets. If you can't bear the thought of missing that upside potential, we will help you refine your exit strategies in Chapter 5.

If you combine the findings of Hypothesis #4 with those of Hypothesis #5, you have a picture of a stock that is trading in a higher range, comes down to a rolling range, then goes

"The will to win is not nearly as important as the will to prepare to win."

—BOBBY KNIGHT

back up. That is a common Rolling Stock pattern. Knowing and understanding that pattern can help you recognize Rolling Stocks and profit from their predictability.

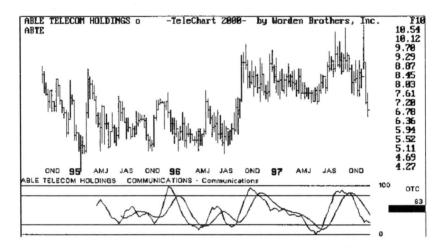

Able Telecom Holdings (ABTE) provides a good example of this long-term pattern. The stock moved from a higher range into a rolling pattern between $5.50 and $6.50. It rolled in that range for over a year. It then moved up into the $7.70 to $9 range and has actually been rolling in that higher range recently.

HYPOTHESIS #6: ROLLING STOCKS TEND TO HAVE PREDICTIVE STOCHASTICS

If I were to pick one analytical tool for identifying a Rolling Stock and helping me make a decision as to when to either buy or sell, that tool would be stochastics. Stochastic displays are featured on TeleChart 2000© and other charting services.

"If you don't have some bad loans you are not in business."
—PAUL VOLCKER

Stochastics is an indicator that measures the price velocity of a stock by sampling price movement over a recent period. The theory behind stochastics is that prices will close near the upper end of a trading range during an uptrend. As the trend matures, prices tend to move away from the upper end of the range. This signals an overbought situation. The converse is true during a downtrend: prices tend to close near the lower end of the trading range. As the stock starts to become over-sold, prices tend to move away from the lower end.

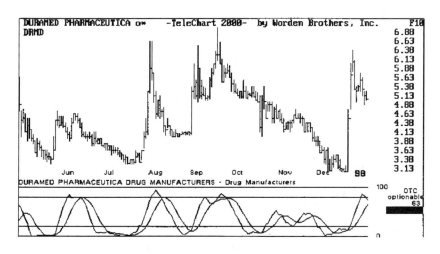

The chart above shows a stochastics indicator in the lower window. This indicator is plotted on a percentage graph. When the stochastic lines are above 80% band, the stock is in the over-bought range and likely to decline. When the stochastic lines are under the 20% band the stock is in the oversold range and likely to go up. When overbought stochastic turns down through its moving average, the indication is to sell. When an

"America is too great for small dreams."

—RONALD REGAN

49

oversold stochastic moves up through its moving average, the signal indicates a buy.

I have closely monitored stochastics as they relate to a stock's movement. For many growth stocks, blue chips, and cyclicals, stochastics are not always a strong predictor of future movement. Stochastics were developed as a tool for futures markets, and as might be expected, they have their greatest predictive power in stocks that are less dependent on news and company fundamentals, and are more likely to move in a range determined by general market conditions.

For Rolling Stocks, stochastics are an excellent predictor of price movement. I generally look for a solid dip below the 20% line as a buy signal. On the exit, I have my GTC to sell in place, but I will defer to a strong stochastic sell signal of 80% or higher. I have found stochastics to be most predictive in Rolling Stocks with a steady average daily volume in excess of 50,000

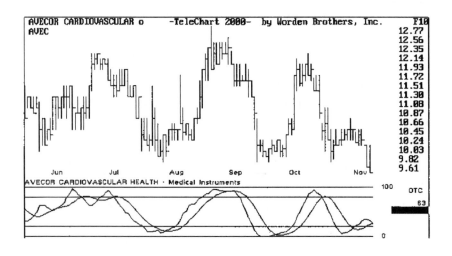

"Knowledge is the only instrument of production that is not subject to diminishing returns."

—JOHN BATES CLARK

shares per day. In low volume stocks the smaller sample makes the indicator less predictive.

The chart of Avecor (AVEC) shows how effective stochastics can be in indicating whether a stock is overbought or oversold. You can also clearly see what a powerful predictor that can be in suggesting what direction the stock is going. As you go looking for Rolling Stocks ready to make their move, let proven analytical tools like stochastics guide you to more profitable trades.

HYPOTHESIS #7: ROLLING STOCKS ARE LESS LIKELY TO BE FOUND IN LARGE, PROFITABLE COMPANIES

I like big, profitable companies with solid earnings increases. I like the feeling I get (and the way I sleep) when I own blue chip stocks and powerhouse growth stocks. I like companies in the habit of "beating the street" when it comes to earnings. I try to populate my portfolio with these types of companies. So it may surprise you to hear that you need to throw those notions out the window when it comes to Rolling Stocks.

But this chapter is about learning to recognize Rolling Stocks by their surroundings. It's about learning to strip away the camouflage and uncover stocks that are in a rolling pattern. Just as camouflage conceals something to make it unnoticeable, marginal profitability and a less than spectacular growth rate can often be a camouflage for a predictable, reliable, and repeatable Rolling Stock.

"A word to the wise ain't necessary—it's the stupid ones who need the advice."

—BILL COSBY

One reason the number of Rolling Stocks tends to be greater among smaller, lesser-known companies is because the market in large blue chip stocks is more efficient. The larger stocks are widely held by institutions. They are actively traded on major exchanges. They are followed religiously by thousands of analysts. Virtually everything there is to know about them is known and absorbed by the market.

Smaller, lesser-known companies on the other hand are more subject to the vagaries of the market. The price is more likely to pop up suddenly or creep up unchecked by the "all-knowing market."

At any given time, I am tracking over 100 Rolling Stocks. I recently checked earnings on each of the stocks I currently track and found that only two of the 107 stocks currently on my watchlist have positive earnings. I have come to accept the fact that Rolling Stocks are a breed of their own. They often defy the rationality of fundamentals and the all-important focus on earnings found in the rest of the market. All I can say is, if you want to make money in Rolling Stocks, get used to it.

WHAT THE RESEARCH TELLS US

As you can see, the research tells us some interesting things about Rolling Stocks and gives us some pretty useful clues as to where to find them. Rolling Stocks often behave differently than the rest of the market. Let's summarize:

- Rolling Stocks tend to be found in the lower price ranges (under $10 per share).

"There are one hundred men seeking security to one able man who is willing to risk his fortune."

—J. PAUL GETTY

- Rolling Stocks generally enter a rolling pattern after coming down from earlier highs.

- After Rolling Stocks complete a rolling pattern, they generally move up to a higher range.

- Stochastics are a good predictor of a Rolling Stock's price movement.

- Rolling Stocks are unlikely to be profitable companies.

Now that we have a better idea of where to find them and how to recognize them, let's learn how to make them work for us in generating cash in our account.

"The individual is the central, rarest, most precious capital resource of our society."

—Peter Drucker

5

SMOOTH ENTRANCES

Once you have identified where the Rolling Stocks are located, then you need to make sure your entrance is timed correctly to achieve your desired return. This chapter is intended to help you pick your buy-in point in a way that maximizes your rate of return.

SHOPPING FOR CARS AND STOCKS

When I'm ready to buy a car, I don't go to just one dealer and hope they have a car I like. I check out as many cars as possible. I'll go to a dozen different lots, view hundreds of cars, and quickly narrow my decision down to maybe a handful of cars from which I can make my decision. Then I do my homework. I scan the literature, talk with friends who may own that car, and check price guides to determine the best price at which I can buy the car.

I use the same process in buying a Rolling Stock. From my list of over 100 Rolling Stocks I select five or 10 that, based on a visual scan of the chart, look like good buy candidates. You should start keeping your own list of potential Rolling Stocks. Then I do my homework. I look at technical factors. What do the stochastics tell me? How is the average daily volume? Has the stock tested its support level? Then I check the fundamentals on each company. I look for news about the company, its

"The successful speculator must be content at times to ignore probably two out of every three apparent opportunities to make money."
—CHARLES DOW

competition, or the sector. Do they have earnings projected? Have their losses been decreasing? If at any point a red flag appears, I eliminate the stock from the pool for this go-around.

Once I've answered those kinds of questions, there are usually one or two stocks that emerge as clear "buy" candidates. I like having two final candidates. I may buy both of them, one of them, or neither. The process up to this point takes me about an hour. By pulling your initial pool of stocks from W.I.N.™ (see Appendix I), you may be able to do it much more quickly.

There is a real hazard in only looking at one stock and trying to make a yes or no decision. French philosopher Emilé Chartier had the right idea when he said, "Nothing is more dangerous than an idea when it's the only one you have." The market is full of opportunity and abounding in great ideas. If you are only working with one potential stock to purchase, you have nothing to compare it to and it's too easy to talk yourself into it.

Let's summarize the steps of how I select my one or two buy candidates, then I'll follow with some specific pointers:

1. Start with a large pool of potential Rolling Stocks.

2. Visually identify between five and 10 that appear to be at or near the trough (support).

3. Evaluate the technical factors.

"It isn't as important to buy as cheap as possible as it is to buy at the right time."

—Jesse Livermore

4. Evaluate the fundamental factors.

5. Narrow the search down to one or two stocks.

RAISING RED FLAGS WITH FUNDAMENTAL ANALYSIS

Before I talk about fundamental analysis, a brief definition may be in order. Fundamental analysis is the study of a company's financial reports, profitability, management, and marketing strategies, as a means of determining the worth of its shares.

Fundamental analysis has severe limits when it comes to low-priced Rolling Stocks. First, there is often little information readily available on many of these stocks. Secondly, since many of these companies do not have a track record of earnings, there is little basis for true valuation. Finally, since our objective with Rolling Stock is to capture small moves repeatedly (say, from $1.50 to $2), fundamental analysis is incapable of pinpointing whether a stock's value is at the top or bottom of a 50¢ range.

For Rolling Stocks I use fundamental analysis to raise red flags and to give me a basic understanding of the company. I do not use it to tell me which stocks to buy, as much as which stocks *not* to buy. Here are some examples of the kinds of serious problems that fundamental analysis can alert you to:

- A prolonged downtrend in revenue

- Decreasing customer base

"Ripeness is all."

—WILLIAM SHAKESPEARE

- Lower same store sales

- High debt/equity ratio

- Negative FCC, FDA or other government regulatory rulings

- Franchisee or dealer disputes

- Lawsuits, particularly those initiated by shareholders (they tend to be especially long, messy, and damaging to a company's stock price)

My first step in fundamental analysis is to go online, either on W.I.N.™ or through other Internet-based resources. If I don't find all the information I'm looking for, I call the company directly and ask for their investor relations contact. I have found that the smaller the company, the more willing this person is to provide you the information you're looking for.

When speaking with the investor relations contact, I identify myself as a private investor interested in obtaining information about their company. I make no mention of their company being a Rolling Stock. I then ask questions about any announced mergers, acquisitions, product rollouts, expansion, et cetera. I ask about expected earnings. I ask if they think the stock is fairly valued at this time. Their answers are often formulaic and even evasive, but what is said, and what goes unsaid, can be revealing.

"In selecting the soundest financial investments, the question of when to buy is far more important than what to buy."
—Roger W. Babson

LET'S GET TECHNICAL

Technical analysis is the study of price, volume, and market sentiment patterns as a means of determining future price movements. Technical analysis is often compared and contrasted to fundamental analysis in a way that suggests the two are contradictory or mutually exclusive. I believe successful investors learn to use the two simultaneously in a way that brings the most useful information to bear on the investment decision.

When it comes to selecting Rolling Stocks, there are some technical indicators that can be valuable. I find that an understanding of trends and the nature of support and resistance are most useful when identifying Rolling Stocks. So let's see if we can come to understand these technical indicators without getting too technical.

Fundamental Analysis *(What to buy)*	**Technical Analysis** *(When to buy)*
Financial reports	Stock Charts
Management	Trading Patterns
Marketing Strategies	Volume
Profitability	Price Trends
Price/Earnings Ratio	Market Sentiment
Products	Support/Resistance
Competition	Moving Averages

"Buy when everyone else is selling and sell when everyone else is buying. This is more than just a catchy slogan. It is the very essence of successful investment."

—J. PAUL GETTY

THE TREND IS YOUR FRIEND

Trends are powerful forces in the marketplace. Analyzing trends is one of the easiest technical tools to grasp. The momentum of a trend is what often drives a bull market to excessive highs and a bear market to such surprising lows. In the study of Rolling Stocks, the trendline helps us identify the support and resistance and enables us to make a more confident buy or sell decision.

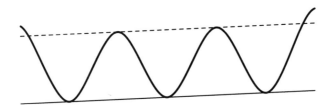

In the illustration above, the trendline on the bottom tracks the support level. Each time the price of the stock touches the trendline, the significance of the trend and the significance of the support level is strengthened. Eventually, the price of the stock breaks through the resistance or support level (this is referred to as a breakout by market technicians). As a stock breaks through the upper trendline, what was once resistance now becomes support. This new support level will usually be tested and established.

We often see the reverse occur as a stock price breaks down below the trendline. In this case, what was once support, now becomes resistance to future upward movement.

"You don't have to be in the business of picking the market bottom or top. Assign the trend to do that job."

—GREGORY WITT

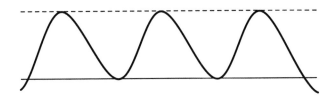

As a buyer of Rolling Stocks, you need to understand where the stock is in relation to the trendline. If the stock price is on its way down to the support level, don't buy until after it has touched that support level, reversed the trend and has begun its ascent back to resistance. For this reason, I generally avoid the practice of putting in a GTC to buy as the stock is on the way down. For example, if a stock that is rolling between $2 and $2.75 is currently priced at $2.25, I would not put in a GTC to buy at $2. The trend could easily take the stock down through support as shown in the example above. I would wind up owning the stock at $2 only to watch it fall to $1.75 or lower. Again, don't buy a stock just because it is approaching support. Make the stock "prove itself" to you by touching support, reversing, and heading upwards. Remember, you don't have to be in the business of picking the market bottom or top. Assign the trend to do that job.

The most commonly used tool in working with trendlines is a moving average. Most stock charting software includes tools for plotting moving averages. Averaging the closing price for a set number of previous days creates a moving average. A chart showing moving averages tends to smooth out the fluctuations found in daily stock charts and gives a more even display of the stock's movement. While I find a moving average to be a

"Behold the turtle. He makes progress only when he sticks his neck out."

—JAMES BRYANT CONANT

useful tool in the analysis of most stocks, I find it to be of limited value in working with Rolling Stocks. The more volatile and fast moving the stock, the less useful a moving average is in a Rolling Stock environment.

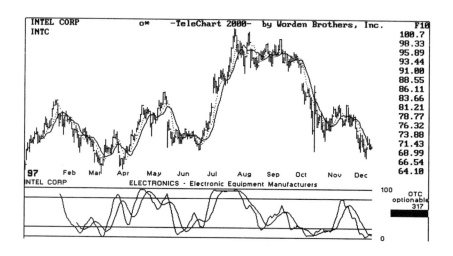

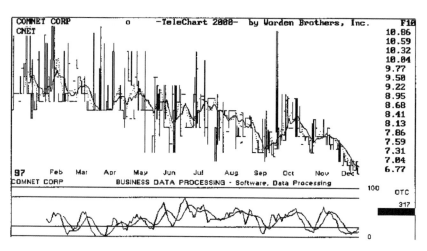

"Business is a continual dealing with the future; it is a continual calculation, an instinctive exercise in foresight."

—HENRY LUCE

The charts on the previous page show both the benefits of using a moving average for most heavily traded stocks, and the limitations of using a moving average for most low-priced Rolling Stocks. Both charts show the price of the stock and two superimposed moving averages, a five-day moving average (shown in the dotted line) and a nine-day moving average (shown in the smoother solid line).

On the chart for Intel (INTC), a strong upward trend is manifest as the shorter-term average (the dotted line) moves away from and above the longer-term (solid line) average. The crossing of the two averages indicates a trend reversal. On the downturn, the shorter-term average falls below the longer-term average as the stock's price falls. Most experienced investors would want to see the downward trend reversed before buying the stock.

The chart for Comnet Corp (CNET), a Rolling Stock marked by low volume and high volatility, shows the futility of using a moving average to pick a buy or sell point. The stock moves so erratically and quickly that any attempt to plot a moving average ends up as a meaningless line drawn somewhere between support and resistance. While this may be an extreme example, it shows how volatility and the speed with which the price fluctuates within the range, can render a moving average useless as an analytical tool for many Rolling Stocks.

As discussed in Chapter 3, stochastics is a powerful indicator for Rolling Stocks. Therefore I look for a stochastic indicator to be near the bottom of the range or under 20 as I am look-

"To understand what is happening today or what will happen in the future, I look back."

—OLIVER WENDELL HOLMES

ing for Rolling Stocks to buy. If I see a stock whose price appears to be at support, but whose stochastic indicator is in the high range, I will exclude it from my pool of candidates.

Not only should the stochastic indicators be in the oversold range, but also there should be a clear indication that the indicator is emerging from that range. I look for the near-term stochastic indicator to be crossing the longer-term indicator and on a decisive uptrend. This is a case where you should never be guilty of trying to read into a chart something that isn't there. Don't assume that because a stochastic indicator is under 20 that it's going to be going up sometime soon.

TURN UP THE VOLUME

Volume refers to the number of shares traded during a given time period. One measure I use in qualifying a Rolling Stock is average daily volume, although you will also see measures of weekly volume or monthly volume. Since the price of a stock is simply an expression of supply and demand, volume is a good indicator of demand, and ultimately, upward movement.

A stock's volume usually moves with the trend. When a stock's volume is steadily increasing, we typically see an upward price movement. In a downtrend we can expect to see declining volume. Reversals are often preceded by a shift in volume. For example, a stock which is advancing on declining volume, suggests a waning of interest and a sign that the stock may be ready for a downturn. Conversely, a stock may be ready

"If you are considering the purchase of a particular stock but aren't happy with the current price, just wait a minute."

—MARKET MAXIM

for an upturn when volume, which has been slow for a period, starts to pick up.

I like to see average daily volume in excess of 50,000 shares a day. This level of volume is evidence of a substantial enough market for technical analysis to have some meaning. It also gives me confidence that there will be liquidity when it comes time for me to sell my shares.

When I see a Rolling Stock with low volume (under 50,000 shares a day, and often much less), I don't read that as a strong negative factor. Instead, it forces me to do more diligent homework. I look more closely at company fundamentals or other factors that are highly favorable. In many of these low volume stocks, the daily volume will fluctuate wildly from one day to the next. As a result, it is very difficult to spot a trend.

If I do choose to invest in these lower volume stocks, I limit my buy to one or two thousand shares. By doing this I not only limit my exposure on a lesser known security, but I find it easier to sell all of my shares when the stock hits the specified sale price.

One rule of thumb that can keep you out of trouble with low volume stocks is to never buy more than 10% of the stock's average daily volume. For example, if the stock has an average daily volume of 50,000 shares, don't buy more than 5,000 shares. This gives you some assurance of liquidity at the time of sale.

"If football taught me anything about business it is that you win the game one play at a time."

—FRAN TARKENTON

Rolling Stocks shown on W.I.N.™ generally have an average daily volume in excess of 70,000 shares per day. This reduces the potential for the market of a low volume stock to be dominated by W.I.N.™ subscribers. To me, this is evidence of information being distributed in a responsible manner by W.I.N.™.

MAKE A MODEL

Once I have narrowed my list of candidates down to one or two stocks, I create a model of how I expect the stock (or stocks) to perform over the next month. When it comes to predicting how the stock will perform in the near term, I have found that the best two predictors are 1) past performance, and 2) the trend. By plotting the expected trendline on the stock chart, using the pattern of previous rolls as a guide, I have developed a simple model of what I expect the stock to deliver in terms of rate of return and duration of roll.

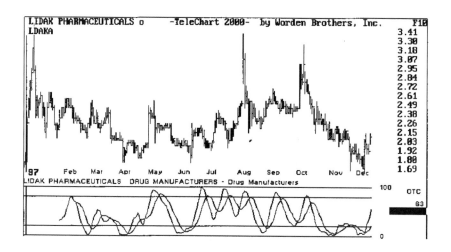

"We can add to our knowledge, but we cannot at will subtract from it."

—ARTHUR KOESTLER

The previous illustration shows how you can quickly and easily create this model and calculate your return:

I don't want anybody to think that this is a difficult procedure. It's not. It should take just a couple of minutes, but will help you understand up front what your entrance, exit, and rate of return should be. Simply plot the trendline from where you intend to buy the stock to where and when you expect to sell the stock. Again, past performance will guide you in determining those two points.

Now determine your expected rate of return. Simply take the cash you expect to get back and divide it by the cash you have tied up in that investment. If you purchased 1,000 shares of stock at $2 per share and expect to sell it at $2.50 the cash you get back would be 50¢ per share or $500. The calculation would look like this:

$$\frac{\text{Profit} = \$500}{\text{Cash invested} = \$2,000} = .25 \text{ or } 25\%$$

Now take a look at the duration of the roll. In this example, we are expecting to sell the stock in one month. That would be a 25% return in one month or a 300% annualized rate of return. If you are comparing two stocks, you may find one with an expected return of 25% in one month, while the other may have a 15% return in a period of two weeks. By annualizing the rate of return, you may choose to give the edge to the 15% return since it turns out to be a 390% annualized rate and it should enable you to get your money out faster for use in another play.

"Every man is a damn fool for at least five minutes every day. Wisdom consists in not exceeding the limit."

—ELBERT HUBBARD

MAKING THE BUY

I make most Rolling Stock purchases by means of a day order. I normally place the order at the predetermined support price. This price may be $1/4$ or $1/8$ below the current ask, but I will often be filled during the course of the day's trading. If I'm not filled by the end of the day, I quickly reevaluate the stock and the order price before trading on the next day. If the basics appear to still be in place, I place the same order the next day. I may make the same order three or even four days in a row until I am filled.

One thing I try to avoid is chasing an entrance. Don't get so enchanted with the purchase of a stock that you chase it up the pole. The homework you did and the logic you applied may not be as valid for a higher entry price. If you think you may still want the stock at the higher price, run through the analysis again. You may find there's another deal waiting in the wings that is sweeter than the one you're chasing.

ALL THAT GLITTERS...

A word about gold and precious metal stocks: I don't consider gold stocks to be Rolling Stocks. Frequently, as I scan charts I see gold and precious metal stocks that appear to have a rolling pattern. What I am really observing is the fluctuation in the value of the metal. The value of most gold and precious metal stocks is so closely tied to the price of the underlying metal, that the market forces and technical fac-

"Leadership cannot really be taught. It can only be learned."
—HAROLD S. GENEEN

tors which drive Rolling Stocks aren't at play in the same way. The moral here is this: buy gold stocks based on company fundamentals and what you expect the price of gold to do. Don't buy them as Rolling Stocks.

Additionally, most gold stocks in the under $5 price range are also small-cap companies. Small-cap gold stocks are fraught with danger and are considerably more risky than the highly capitalized and well-established gold mining companies listed on the New York Stock Exchange and NASDAQ.

Seasonal Factors

I find that December is a difficult month to go shopping for great Rolling Stocks. Market analysts refer to this as the "December Effect." There are year-end factors such as tax selling and institutional "house cleaning" happening around the end of the year. This makes fast turnarounds and normal technical factors go awry.

The January effect typically gives a boost to low-priced and small company stocks. I find consistent success in buying Rolling Stocks during January. Summer months are generally favorable. However, when the signals are right I make a buy regardless of the season.

"Never mistake motion for action."

—Ernest Hemingway

6

MANAGING THE CLIMB

While teaching stock strategies, I have the opportunity to watch investors make decisions and either profit from the results or suffer the consequence. There is a difference between successful and unsuccessful investors, how they view the market, and how they approach trading. Successful investors are more decisive by nature. They take full responsibility for their decisions and they are quick to take their profits or cut their losses.

The less successful investors view themselves at the mercy of the market. They view any potential gain or loss as the result of luck. Their most common lament is "I just don't know what went wrong." As a result of not acting decisively, they turn to hope as a means of reversing an unfavorable position. Hope is a wonderful virtue, but it has no impact on the price of a stock. These investors then move on to another losing investment without ever knowing or even assessing what went wrong.

MANAGING VS. BABY SITTING

When it comes to investing are you a manager or a baby sitter? When I speak of baby sitters I'm not talking about a truly great baby sitter like my daughter Lindsey (she's hard working, dedicated, and CPR certified). No, I'm talking about the

"Sometimes we stare so long at a door that is closing that we see too late the one that is open."

—ALEXANDER GRAHAM BELL

careless, lazy, baby sitters who feel that since they are under-paid, it is their right to sit around watching television while the kids finger-paint the floor with ketchup and plug the toilet with a Nerf ball. They don't have a clue as to what is happening. They may do some yelling and make a few threats, but they have no control over the kids they are tending.

There are people who handle their investments with a baby sitting mentality. They invest in whatever comes along. They make the investment decision carelessly, with insufficient analysis and attention to the stock's fundamentals or technical factors. They are content with a 10% annual return (that's underpaid). They rarely cut their losses. Instead, they whine or complain to their broker. They lack the decisiveness to take control of the situation.

They are dabbling in the stock market. Unfortunately for them, the stock market doesn't treat dabblers kindly. The size and sophistication of our nation's financial markets require that to be successful, you must treat it like a business.

Contrast the baby sitting approach to that of the professional manager. The manager knows that his primary responsibility is to generate a return on investment. That investment may be time, money, or human resources. Planning and organization are critical to success. The success of the organization depends on the decision making of its managers. Those decisions include investing in the right resources and hiring and developing the right people. And, when needed, taking necessary corrective action.

"Capitalism without bankruptcy is like Christianity without hell."
—FRANK BORMAN

People who *manage* their investment portfolio are in control of their resources. They make their investment selections by gathering data, analyzing the information, then using their judgment and experience to arrive at a decision. Once the decision is made, they don't walk away and neglect it. They carefully monitor the results of their decision, and if it becomes necessary, they will make needed course corrections. They take seriously the market maxim to "control what you can, and manage what you cannot."

CONTROL WHAT YOU CAN, MANAGE WHAT YOU CANNOT

What are some of the things you as an investor can *control*?

- What you buy

- Whether or not you buy

- When you buy

- Where you buy

- Who you buy from

- Why you buy

- How long you hold your investment

- When you sell

- Why you sell

- What you do with your earnings

"In the business world, everyone is paid in two coins: cash and experience. Take the experience first; the cash will come later."
—HAROLD S. GENEEN

These are the areas where you need to exercise complete control. Ultimately, *you* have control over the *most important* aspects of your investment. The outcome (whether you make money or lose money) has more to do with *you* and how you control your part of the process than with the other market factors.

There are certainly factors over which you have no control, but they play a lesser role than many investors think. These are the factors you *manage*:

- What happens to the price of the stock after you buy

- News

By *manage*, I mean you adjust your game plan to take into account the circumstances you are faced with. Once you have exercised control by making the decision, then you review and revise your plan as the circumstances (those things over which you have no control) change.

Rolling Stocks were never meant to be a "no brainer." Just because you've bought the right stock at the right time doesn't mean you can put in your GTC and walk away. You need to keep abreast of your positions and be ready to act on the information you receive.

I normally monitor every position in my portfolio at least once a day. I do this on my laptop computer either by updating TeleChart 2000© or by connecting to the Internet and scanning my stocks using current quotes on W.I.N.™. If I don't have easy

---

"Failure is good. It's fertilizer. Everything I've learned about coaching, I've learned from making mistakes."
—RICK PITINO

access to the Internet, I can always call my broker on the toll-free number and get the quotes I need.

SETTING THE STOP

In addition to putting in a GTC order to sell your stock at the desired peak price, you can also establish the stop point. A stop order is a limit order to protect you from significant losses. If the price of your shares declines to the level set in your stop order, it becomes an active order that is executed.

Stop orders take two different forms, a *stop order* or a *stop limit order*. With a stop order you specify a price which becomes the trigger. As soon as the specified price is reached, your order becomes a market order and the stock will sell immediately. A stop limit order is similar to a stop order, but instead of turning into a market order when your price is reached, your order becomes a limit order at the specified price.

With a stop limit order the price must be met for the stock to sell. You should be aware that your stop limit order may not fill even if the stock reaches the limit price, since all limit orders are filled in sequence by the exchanges. If the price changed before the exchange reaches your order (due to the number of previous orders or your order size), your order may not fill.

While I always have a GTC in for the sell, I do not use a stop order on the downside. Instead, I set a "mental stop," that is, I determine that point at which I will sell. If the stock drops to that point, I spend about ten minutes reviewing the

"You only have to do a very few things right in your life so long as you don't do too many things wrong."
—WARREN BUFFETT

75

chart, reassessing the fundamentals, and unless there are clear, compelling reasons to hold on to the stock, I make the sale. In my case, that normally takes place online. If you were trading with a full service broker, you would want to call and get his recommendation.

I use mental stops because most brokers will not permit you to "put a noose" around a stock, that is, place a GTC to sell both on the upside as well as the downside. You may want to ask your broker if they permit such an order. Brokers often refer to it as an OCO (one cancels the other) order.

Here's how an OCO order works. Let's say you buy a stock at $10 a share. You place a GTC to sell at $12 for a 20% return. At the same time you can place another GTC as a stop order to sell at $9, should the stock decline to that point. Whichever sell point the stock hits first will become the active order, and the other order is canceled.

It makes little difference whether you use a mental stop, a stop order, or an OCO order. The intent and the result are the same. You need to be disciplined and decisive enough to know where you are prepared to cut your losses. When I say that you need to know when to get out, understand that the rule applies to both the upside as well as the downside.

Now comes the tough question: where do you put the stop? Your stop should be a function both of what you expect to gain and what your downside potential is. If you open a position

"Sometimes your best investments are the ones you don't make."
—DONALD TRUMP

with an expected roll of 30%, I would keep my stop loss well inside the 30% range, typically at half that or 15%.

Using that rule of thumb, if you purchased a stock at $2, which rolled in a range of $2 to $2.75 your expected rate of return would be 38%. You would set a stop loss of no more than half of that expected return, or 19%. Using your buy price of $2 less 18%, the most you would be willing to lose would be 38¢. Therefore, your stop order would be placed no lower than $1.62. This stop order prevents your losses on any one stock from diminishing your trading capital beyond what one or two subsequent plays are able to recoup.

Remember, the above rule of thumb identifies the maximum you are willing to lose. You should be watching any losing position carefully. If a position dips below your buy price, assess the fundamentals and technicals to see if you would still buy it knowing what you know now. If not, consider selling. The stock market adage "cut your dogs loose, and let your eagles soar" reminds us that losing positions often get worse before they get better.

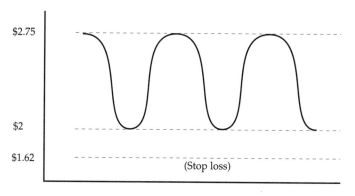

"A stock doesn't know you own it."

—WARREN BUFFETT

Managing Your Position On The Climb

Enough of the bad news. Now let's turn our attention to the profit side of the equation and learn what you can do to manage your profits and maximize your return on the upside.

In addition to placing stop orders to cut your losses, you can also set trailing stops as the stock price increases as a means of protecting your profits. For example, you might have bought 1,000 shares of Trusted Information Systems (TISX) at $8.87 on September 4th when the buy signals were strongest. Once you were filled, you put in a GTC to sell at $13 for a 46% rate of return.

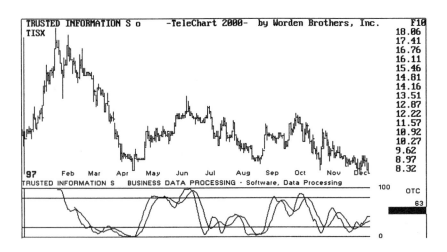

By late September the stochastics had given a sell signal and the stock price started to edge slightly lower. Even though you expected the stock to eventually go higher, you could have

---

"No price is too low for a bear or too high for a bull."
—Market Maxim

changed your GTC to a stop order as a means of preserving your profits. If you sold on September 29th at $10, you still would have realized a 12% rate of return for less than a month.

The price of TISX subsequently reached a high of $12 (which would have given you a tasty 35% return) but failed to reach its previous peak of $13. The roll was flattening out (a pattern we frequently see after one or two mega-rolls) and you would have been better off taking a less-than-expected profit, rather than hold out as the stock slides back below your original entry price of $8.87.

LEARN THE TECHNICAL SELL SIGNS

The best technical indicator for predicting both the buy point and the sell point for a Rolling Stock is stochastics. But since stochastics is based on a historical sampling and moving average, it will always lag the actual movement of the stock based on the period settings.

For many Rolling Stocks with an even roll this lag does not pose a problem. But for stocks with a more volatile roll, or which tend to spike up and down, the lag in the indicator is a serious deficiency. The following two charts give a good visual picture of two different patterns found in Rolling Stocks: *rollers* and *spikers.*

Here is a classic roller. The chart for Criticare Systems (CXIM) shows a fairly predictable, even roll with steady climbs and steady descents. In this type of pattern, stochastics are a powerful predictor. It may not always pick the absolute top or

"Take care to sell your horse before he dies. The art of life is passing losses on."

—ROBERT FROST

bottom of the chart, but as long as you're not greedy, you'll still make a great rate of return.

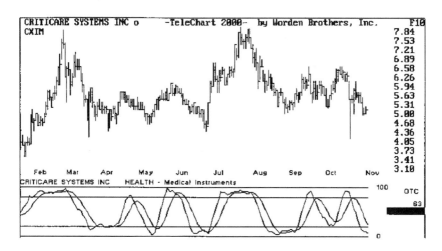

Now for a textbook example of a spiker: Cellex Biosciences (CLXX) makes most of its upward moves in a spike often lasting just a day or two. Then it quickly retreats to a lower level. If you want to play this as a Rolling Stock, don't go looking to stochastics as your guide. The sell signal from stochastics generally comes a few days after the stock has made its fall.

In the absence of a reliable sell signal, the best you can do is to set a *reasonable* GTC for the sell. By reasonable, I would set it a few percentage points below the previous peak. In the case of CLXX, if you had bought it on August 29th at $1.69 when the stochastic buy signals first appeared, you could have looked to previous rolls of 25% and greater and set your GTC accordingly.

"Everything comes to him who hustles while he waits."
—THOMAS EDISON

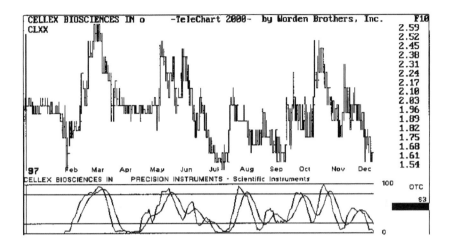

But because it's a spiker, and doesn't give you reliable sell signals, you would have been perfectly justified in placing your GTC at 20% rather than 25%. At a 20% return your GTC would have filled three days later on August 21st. The stock continued to climb for another three days before making its retreat.

In summary, while there is no perfect sell signal, you should be able to obtain the most reliable and optimal profit by using a combination of stochastics and the historic rolling pattern of the stock to make your sell decision. For stocks with a smoother roll (rollers), give the greater weight to stochastics. When stocks have a more volatile, spiking pattern (spikers) base your decision more on the historic rate of return.

DON'T LET THE RANGE RIDE YOU

When you are in control of your money and when you are managing your investments, information then becomes your

"A study of economics usually reveals that the best time to buy anything is usually last year."

—MARTY ALLEN

tool. On the other hand, when you are not in control of your money and when you are baby sitting your investments, information becomes your master.

For many novice Rolling Stock investors there is a tendency to think of the rolling range as immovable. They buy the stock, determine the sale price, put in the GTC, and never adjust their game plan after that. Remember, *you are in control of the range.* You determine what the bottom and top of the range are. You are the one riding the range. *Don't let the range ride you.*

NEVER SELL SIMPLY BECAUSE OF A RUN-UP

I like taking my profits as much as anybody. I am quick to take profits, particularly in options trading. Because options expire and have a time value that is constantly diminishing prior to expiration, there is good justification to take profits quickly. I have frequently left money on the table by selling an option at a nice profit only to watch the option go on to make an even better profit.

But unlike options, Rolling Stocks don't expire and don't have an eroding time value. As a result, I don't feel as pressured to sell Rolling Stocks in order to claim a quick profit. I avoid the temptation to sell my stock just because it has had a nice run-up. Instead, I wait for the stock to reach the peak of its historic roll while watching along the way for sell signals.

Simply put, there are three times when I will sell a Rolling Stock.

"A man who wants to test the depth of the river doesn't put in both legs at the same time."

—AFRICAN PROVERB

1. When it reaches previously established resistance.

2. When it generates a sell signal based on stochastics.

3. When it fails to meet profit expectations by either not moving in the right direction or not moving in a timely manner.

If you sell simply because the stock has had a few strong days, you are acting on greed or fear. All too often, the decision is not based on solid analysis and the result will be profits left on the table.

BEWARE OF SHIFTS IN MARKET PSYCHOLOGY

Significant shifts in market psychology or in the fundamentals of the stock require that you change your game plan. Here are a few examples of how that shift could alter your strategy.

Good News. Low-priced and lesser known stocks can be particularly sensitive to news. New products, successful completion of clinical trials, positive sector news, positive earnings, potential mergers, and new management, can all have a positive and dramatic impact on the price of the stock.

When this happens I prefer to cancel my GTC as quickly as possible and see where the news takes me. The result is almost always positive. The chart for Cypros Pharmaceutical (CYPR) shows what happens to the price of a biotechnology firm as they announce positive trial results on three of their products in development during October 1997. The

---

"I'd be a bum on the street with a tin cup if the markets were always efficient."

—WARREN BUFFETT

stock price doubled. After a period of consolidation at the top, it headed back down.

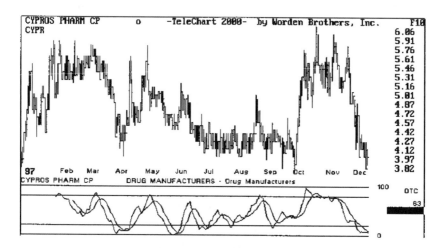

Obviously, bad news can have a dramatic negative impact on the price of a Rolling Stock. In the face of bad news I prefer to change my GTC to a market order to sell the stock quickly as a means of preserving my profit.

Support becomes resistance. The key to success in the Rolling Stock strategy lies in learning to identify support and resistance. Once you've learned to identify support and resistance you can make profitable Rolling Stock transactions. But your long-term success and profitability often lies in learning to read sudden shifts in market psychology. During these shifts the price of a stock can fall below its previous level of support or move above its previous level of resistance. The result is a breakout.

"The most difficult part of getting to the top of the ladder is getting through the crowd at the bottom."

—ARCH WARD

Once the breakout occurs, the previous support or resistance level has been broken, and for all practical purposes, done away with. When a stock breaks out to the upside, the price which was resistance now becomes a new support level for the stock to test and establish. Likewise, when a stock breaks out below support, the previous support level now becomes resistance for a new, lower trading range.

This type of shift in market psychology requires that you be ready to move quickly by either canceling your GTC to take advantage of greater upside potential, or selling quickly to protect yourself from loss.

Reversals. A reversal occurs when a rolling pattern or a pattern of upward movement changes in a downward direction. One of the more common reversal patterns is known by market technicians as a "head and shoulders" reversal.

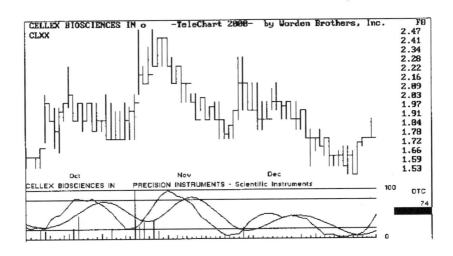

"If you hear that everybody is buying a certain stock, ask who is selling."

—JAMES DINES

The head and shoulders reversal consists of a large, more broadly sustained roll (head) flanked on both sides by smaller rallies (shoulders) followed by a breakout. One of the most reliable indicators of an impending breakout is that the right shoulder is formed under low volume, indicating a weakness in the rally and the likelihood of breakout to the downside.

The chart for Cellex (CLXX) shows a clear example of the head and shoulders pattern. Although the size and length of the shoulders may vary, the low volume on the right shoulder is present and the breakout to the low end occurs.

How Long Can This Go On?

All good things must come to an end, and Rolling Stocks are no exception. But as support and resistance continue to be tested over time, the strength of the pattern is actually reinforced. The longer the roll continues, the more substantial it is. Also, the longer the roll continues, the more powerful the following breakout will be. The market will continue to hold to that pattern until some significant events or changes force a breakout.

If you are doing your homework and waiting for the appropriate buy signals, you should be able to shield yourself from a sudden breakout on the downside. The greatest risk, then, occurs in selling your stock before it breaks out to the upside.

As the stock approaches the sell point, take a few minutes to reevaluate the price of the stock, the strength of the trend,

---

"If you don't know where you are going, you will probably end up somewhere else."

—LAURENCE J. PETER AND RAYMOND HULL

and other technical and fundamental factors which could push the price of the stock higher. If positive signs are in place (even if there is no significant positive news), I often cancel my GTC and avoid rushing in to take profits. Or, to put it another way, if it ain't broke, don't sell it.

"Forecasts usually tell us more of the forecaster than of the future."
—WARREN BUFFETT

7

SYNCOPATED ROLLS: A POWER STRATEGY

Until now, I've been talking as if you purchase a stock, ride it up, sell it, and wait for it to go back down. Now I'm going to give you a technique that has the potential to more than double the returns that Rolling Stocks can generate in your portfolio.

I first developed this power strategy as I was watching a number of my Rolling Stocks make their descent back to the buy range. I made a simple, but powerful observation (I've come to recognize that most powerful principles are generally quite simple at their root). I noticed that most Rolling Stocks took longer to come down than they took to go up. Our example from Chapter 2, Just Toys Inc. (ticker JUST) provides solid proof of this observation.

Just Toys (JUST)	Climb	Descent to 1st Buy	Descent to Best Buy
Roll 1	5 days	41 days	57 days
Roll 2	4	68	111
Roll 3	12	19	23
Roll 4	2	17	17
Roll 5	24	18	31
Roll 6	13	7	31
Roll 7	10	n/a	n/a
Average of rolls 1-6	17 days	28 days	36 days

"Bear markets have no supports, and bull markets have no resistance."

—WILLIAM F. ENG

The above graph for Just Toys shows under the heading "Climb" the number of trading days from the day the stochastics gave the strongest buy signal until the day the stock would have been sold using a GTC at $2. Under "Descent to 1st Buy" is the number of days from the sale of the stock to the first day on which you could have purchased the stock at $1.25 (the support line or bottom of our rolling range). "Descent to Best Buy" shows the number of days from the sale to the time when the price was at or below $1.25 and the stochastics and other technical indicators gave the strongest buy signals.

In this example, on average, the stock took twice as long to make the descent as it took to make the climb. The typical holding period for the stock was just 17 days, while the typical waiting period to get back in was 36 days.

I then went on to study the charts of hundreds of Rolling Stocks and found the same basic pattern to be evident in the vast majority of companies. The rise is generally faster than the fall. This seemed to defy nature!

I admit that I was surprised to see such a pattern, since the same is not the case with trending stock. Stocks with a strong uptrend generally take longer to climb and then get slammed in a sudden plunge.

Now for the moral of the story: *don't let grass grow under your feet*. In the time you are waiting for the stock to make its slide back down to the buy range, put your cash to work with another Rolling Stock. This is what I call *"syncopated rolls."*

"Opportunity is a moving target, and the bigger the opportunity, the faster it moves."

—Richard Gaylor Briley

Syncopated rolls can best be understood by plotting two Rolling Stocks side by side. As soon as stock ABC is sold, stock XYZ is purchased. While stock ABC is making its descent, stock XYZ is making its climb. In its simplest form it could look something like this:

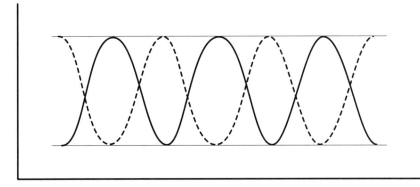

Stock ABC (solid line)   Stock XYZ (dotted line)

As soon as stock ABC is sold, you buy stock XYZ. As stock ABC is making its long, slow descent, stock XYZ is making its meteoric rise. You've just doubled your rate of return.

If you can roll two stocks simultaneously, is it possible to manage three at the same time? Could you really keep three stocks rolling in syncopated rolls using the same trading capital? Yes, but that's about as far as you can usually make it stretch.

Now you're probably saying to yourself, "That's impossible!" You may think it's inconceivable that three, or even two, stocks could have the same rolling frequency and be staggered

---

"Don't confuse brains with a bull market."

—HUMPHREY NEILL

in perfect harmony so as to make a syncopated roll possible. You're right. I've never seen it happen.

But using the same trading capital and a collection of only ten or so active Rolling Stocks within a given price range, you will find that as soon as one stock peaks out, there is another stock waiting in the wings to make its climb. By selling one stock and cycling another stock in as soon as the buy signals are right, you can effectively run two or even three stocks in syncopated rolls.

In the process, by using the *same trading capital,* you can easily *double* and *potentially triple* the returns you would get if you only rolled one stock at a time. That is the power of syncopated rolls!

To do this successfully, you must have a group of 10 or more active Rolling Stocks within the same price range. TeleChart 2000© or other charting software packages have watchlists which enable you to easily cluster stocks in whatever categories you choose. You can run sorts and create multiple watchlists of favorite automotive stocks, for example, or stocks that have been advancing five days in a row, or stocks with closing prices between $1.50 and $1.75.

I would suggest having a group or watchlist of Rolling Stocks that trade in the under $5 range, and another watchlist of stocks trading in the $5 to $10 range. This should give you plenty of stocks to work with and yet only have two lists to manage. You could fine tune this process and have stocks sorted

---

"If you don't invest very much, then defeat doesn't hurt very much and winning is not very exciting."

—DICK VERMEIL

in increments of $2, but that might be too much work with no additional time saving or efficiency.

In each watchlist you could easily monitor 10 to 20 stocks at a time. As soon as one stock in that price range sells, you quickly scan your list to see which of the other stocks in that price range is ready for a buy. With a group of 10 or more stocks to choose from there is bound to always be one in the buy range or within a week of a buy at any given time.

How do you populate your watchlists? Here are several easy ways:

- Every week W.I.N.™ publishes a list of 15 to 20 Rolling Stocks. Just put those stocks into your watchlist. That will get you off to a great start.

- Once a month do a scan of all stocks in a certain price range, for example, all stocks between $2 and $3. Sort through the scan results quickly to look for Rolling Stocks. I can generally review about 20 stocks a minute and make a visual assessment as to whether the stock is rolling. This whole process will take less than an hour, but the results will astound you. You should easily be able to add 10 or more Rolling Stocks to your watchlist every time you do this scan.

- As you come across stocks in the news or hear about companies in your area, check their chart. Once you make a habit of looking for Rolling Stocks, you'll be sur-

"It's only when the tide goes out that you learn whose been swimming naked."

—WARREN BUFFETT

prised how many you find. As you find these stocks, add them to your watchlist.

Every couple of months you can purge your watchlist. Eliminate those stocks that are no longer rolling. Delete those that have had a breakout to a new higher range or that have had a breakdown to a new lower range.

The alternative to purging your watchlist of stocks no longer rolling is to let those stocks stay in your watchlist with the hope they might start rolling again. It may take you a little extra time to sort through them every week or so, but you'll be amazed at how many of these stocks keep reappearing in a rolling pattern over time.

This whole process of managing watchlists and syncopating rolls takes no more than 15 or 20 minutes a day. If you are already actively managing a portfolio, you can add the Rolling Stock management techniques described in this chapter in just a few minutes a day. I know of no more profitable way to spend your time than to supercharge your Rolling Stocks into a cash flow money machine.

"The bottom line is in heaven."

—EDWIN HERBERT LAND

8

CASE STUDIES

Now that you have learned techniques for finding, selecting, and entering Rolling Stocks, let's spend some time honing our skills by reviewing a few charts. Since much of your success in Rolling Stocks will come from your ability to read and interpret charts, I've selected charts that require you to apply the techniques we've discussed so far.

As you review the charts and the analysis, watch for patterns. Watch for the predictable trends, movements and features you can transfer to other stocks you are monitoring. Successful investors are usually keen observers.

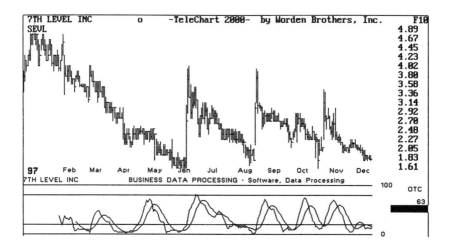

7th Level (SEVL) is a software company that produces CD-ROM-based interactive entertainment and educational software for home computers. The stock was trading in the $10 to $15 range for much of 1996 then slumped into the under $5 range during 1997. It provides a textbook example of how a Rolling Stock generally enters a rolling range after dropping from a higher level. I purchased 7th Level at $1.78 and put in a GTC to sell at $3 for a 68% return.

It also provides an unmistakable visual picture of how Rolling Stocks frequently spike up, then take a much longer time to roll back down again. On a spiker like this, stochastics are less reliable. There were several instances during 1997 when they gave a clear and accurate buy signal, but there were also some erratic stochastics and false buy signals.

"Fortune does not change men; it only unmasks them."
—MADAM RICCOBONI

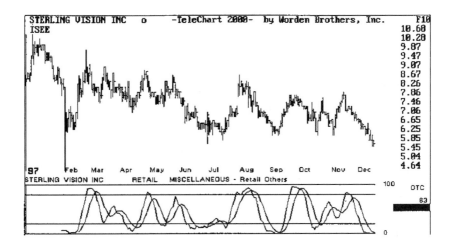

Sterling Vision (ISEE) is a large retail and franchised optical store chain with about 350 outlets in the US and Canada. They have traded between $5 and $10 for the past two years. For the second half of 1997 they established a nice roll between $6 and $7.50.

The even roll moves quickly, but without the spikes and erratic behavior of some Rolling Stocks. This is a good example of a roll that is best predicted by stochastics.

Even though there is a pronounced downtrend over the course of the year, there was an excellent return for those who followed the formulas. Those who did so also were able to shield themselves from the stock's year-end decline.

"It is far better to sleep on what you plan to do, than stay awake because of what you have done."

—WADE B. COOK

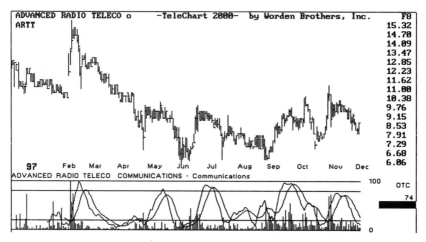

Advanced Radio Telecom (ARTT) provides wireless services to telecommunications providers using microwave transmissions. The company had an IPO (Initial Public Offering) at $15 in November 1996. It then moved down to roll in a range under $10 for the second half of 1997.

They rolled between $6.50 and $9 with good regularity. Because pricing of an IPO is more an art than a science, there is often a shakeout which occurs in the first few months as the market sifts hype from reality. In the case of ARTT, this happened fairly quickly and the stock moved into a more comfortable trading range, providing a 30%+ rate of return on each roll.

ARTT shows the typical December slide and January boost that occurs in many low priced Rolling Stocks. By studying the daily volume, there is also clear evidence of a stock which builds a trend on steadily increasing volume and declines on lower volume.

"Fortune knocks at every man's door once in a life, but in many cases the man is in a neighboring saloon and does not hear her."
—MARK TWAIN

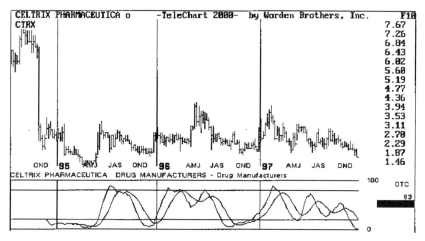

Celtrix Pharmaceuticals (CTRX) develops drugs for the treatment of degenerative conditions such as osteoporosis and multiple sclerosis. The stock was trading in the $7 to $10 range until late 1994 when a product setback slammed the stock into the under $5 range.

Biotechnology stocks are highly speculative since sizable profits hinge on the FDA approval process. I try to avoid "one-trick dogs" in my portfolio. I like to look at companies like CTRX that have strategic alliances with other manufactures and have several products in development. These companies often go into a rolling pattern after they have been rejected on a particular drug. They also provide some interesting upside potential should the approval process work in their favor.

Throughout most of 1997, stochastics were a good predictor of upward movement in the stock price. However, by year-end the stock was trending down and the stochastics were erratic and inconclusive. This was a good signal to stay out.

"Quit tripping over pennies on your way to dollars."

—WADE B. COOK

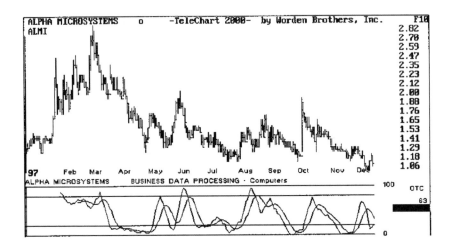

Alpha Microsystems (ALMI) gives us a good example of what I call a "flattening roll." The pattern begins with a big roll that produces a 50 to 100% rate of return. The subsequent rolls become more moderate and tend to flatten out over time. Market technicians refer to this pattern as a Descending Triangle Reversal, but I prefer just calling it as I see it, thus, a "flattening roll."

The positive side of this pattern is that the support level tends to remain intact, while the resistance level adjusts downward. This kind of chart makes it difficult to pick your exit, but you can still get good buy signals and avoid some downside risk.

"Sometimes the best gain is to lose."
—FRANCOIS DUC DE LA ROCHEFOUCAULD

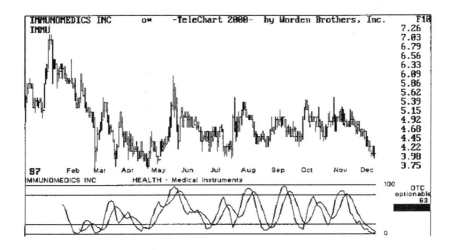

Immunomedics, Inc. (IMMU) is another example of a bio-technology company with more than five products in various stages of development. The stock roll regularly between $4.25 and $5.00 for an average return of 17% per roll.

The roll is consistent and responds predictably to stochastic buy and sell signals. It also seems to have suffered from the December sell-off common among lower priced stocks, but was showing strength through January.

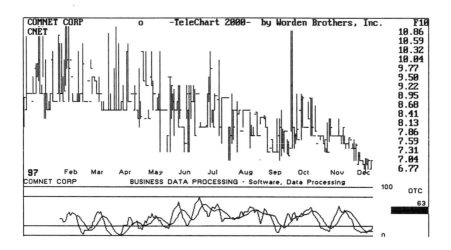

The chart for Comnet Corp. (CNET) is more interesting than the company. It shows the effects of low volume on the stock's volatility. A typical daily trading range varied 10% between the high and the low. And trading ranges with a 20% difference between high and low are not uncommon. This is not just a bid/ask spread, but actual movement in the stock's price during the trading day.

By trading in low volume (1,000 shares or less per day) you can make some consistent small profits. But beware. Technical analysis tools such as stochastics and relative strength are meaningless in such a low volume stock.

"The true way to gain much is never to desire to gain too much."
—FRANCIS BEAUMONT

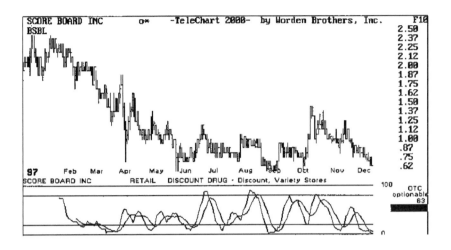

The Score Board (BSBL) produces and sells sports and en-tertainment memorabilia. They have had rapid growth, al-though earnings have been negative. With a roll between 75¢ and $1, this is definitely at the low end of the price spectrum.

Remember, the lower the price of the stock, the more likely you are to have higher rolls. My plan here is to catch the rolling pattern in what appears to be its initial phases. I have successfully rolled this for a 33% return and hope to see it roll for months to come.

With a stock under $1 stochastics still proves to be a useful indicator. The signal is faint, but consistently accurate.

"The best throw with the dice is to throw them away."

—CHARLES SIMMONS

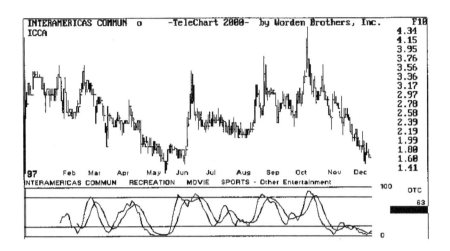

I have fun playing companies with charts like this. They have big rolls, and they take more patience, since the rolls are farther apart and not as predictable. Also, the timing and technical factors are more difficult to work with. But the rate of return makes it all worthwhile.

Interamericas Communication Corp. (ICCA) had several rolls each with a return of 75% or more during 1997. The rolls didn't have the same entry point, so you need to watch the stock and adjust to current conditions. While it finished the year suffering from the December effect common to many Rolling Stocks, it looks poised to repeat a rolling pattern again.

The message on ICCA is to be on the lookout for shifts in market conditions. Don't be governed by the range. Instead, be flexible and capable of altering the range when the technical and fundamental picture changes.

"A man there was, and they called him mad; the more he gave, the more he had."

—JOHN BUNYAN

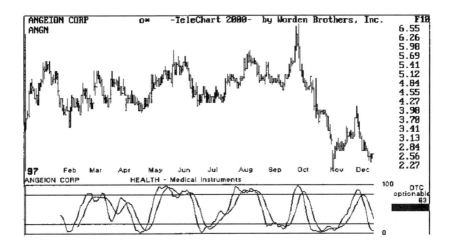

Here's a good lesson in not buying a stock just because it hit the bottom of the roll. Remember to wait for the buy signals. Had you bought Angeion Corp. (ANGN) in October just before the mini-crash of 1997, you would have taken a loss.

As the stock fell through its support level of $4.20, the breakdown took it to a new support level of around $2.50. The old support level of $4.20 now becomes the new resistance level and it starts another profitable rolling pattern. At the end of 1997 the rolling range was comfortable between $2.50 and $3.50.

"Genius is nothing but continued attention."

—CLAUDE ADRIEN HELVETIUS

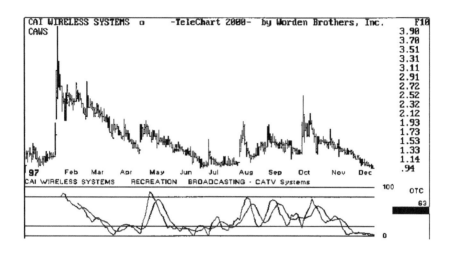

CAI Wireless (CAWS) gives us just one more example of a stock which traded for several years in the $10 range. But through most of 1997 it provided nice 20%+ rolls in the $1 range.

Even though the rolling pattern wasn't exactly predictable or repeatable, I bought CAWS in late December at $1 and put in a GTC for a 50% rate of return. It started to go up and everything seemed to be working according to plan.

Within a week of purchasing the stock I noticed that on one particular day the trading volume was shown to be zero. That was a red flag that something was wrong. I quickly called their investor relations agent and found that the stock had been taken off NASDAQ and was now trading on the OTC bulletin board. The stock had been taken off NASDAQ because it failed to meet the exchange's capitalization and price standards. I sold at a loss, but felt that I was better off putting my money somewhere else than waiting for a long-term turnaround.

"To accept good advice is but to increase one's own ability."
—JOHANN WOLFGANG VON GOETHE

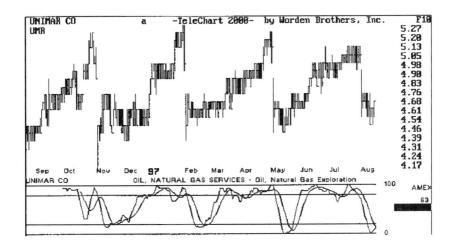

At first glance, Unimar (UMR) looks like the most religious rolling chart you've ever seen. But looks can be deceiving. Instead, this is a company with a $5 stock paying a 45¢ quarterly dividend. At the payment of each dividend, the market discounts the price of the stock.

This is just a lesson to reinforce the point that you need to be familiar with the company fundamentals. Otherwise, you could have bought a nice dividend yield, without the more aggressive cash flow and upside potential of a true Rolling Stock.

"All business proceeds on beliefs, or judgments of probabilities, and not on certainties."

—CHARLES W. ELIOT

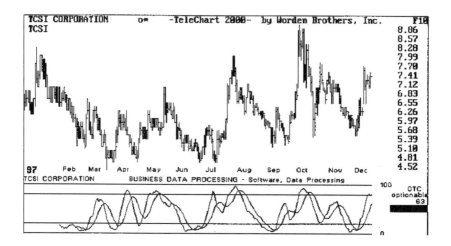

TCSI Corp. (TCSI) shows us that you don't always have to pick the top of a roll to get a great rate of return. You could have taken a 30% return on several occasions. Sure, there were also several opportunities for a 60% or more rate of return, but the lower return was more predictable and frequent.

The chart also shows the upward trend of a range rider. Notice how support has shifted from $4.50 up to $5.50. Likewise, resistance has increased from $7 to $9.

"Markets as well as mobs respond to human emotions; markets as well as mobs can be inflamed to their own destruction."

—OWEN D. YOUNG

9

RANGE RIDERS

After you've been a student of Rolling Stocks for a year, and have learned to generate monthly returns of 10 to 20% on a consistent basis, you will be rewarded with a few range riders. Going back to Wade Cook's cab driver experience, Rolling Stocks are like the little $3 and $4 taxi fares around town. You'll make a great return on these little "meter drops." But range riders are the big trips to the airport.

A range rider is a stock that has a repeating pattern of highs and lows on its price range and gradually rises to a successively higher range over time. Range riders can best be visualized by taking a Rolling Stock and slanting it in an upward direction. We can also give it a downward slant and then it becomes a "reverse range rider."

Rolling Stock

Range Rider

Reverse Range Rider

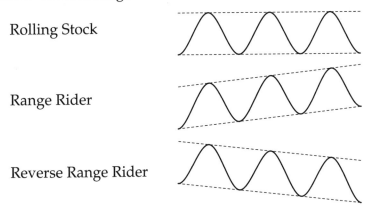

"To turn $100 into $110 is work. To turn $100 million into $110 million is inevitable."

—EDGAR BRONFMAN

I like to think of range riders as Rolling Stocks that have graduated. I have chosen to include this chapter because range riders are really just hybrid Rolling Stocks. My experience with range riders shows that most of them emerge from a rolling pattern and then begin to make their longer, more sustained ascent.

As I've studied the patterns of range riders, I've found that they rarely spike up to a new, higher level. Instead, they continue the rolling pattern, but in a pronounced upward direction. Their long sustained climb is often characterized by dips along the way, but the dips rarely break below the previous resistance level or moving average.

We see good examples of range riders in all price ranges. The charts of Iomega (IOM) and AT&T (T) are textbook examples of range riders. But because of their higher price (Iomega

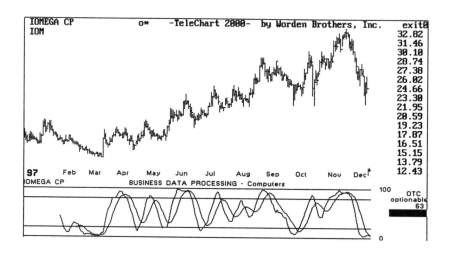

"The obvious rarely gets you anywhere in the stock market."
—KENNETH L. FISHER

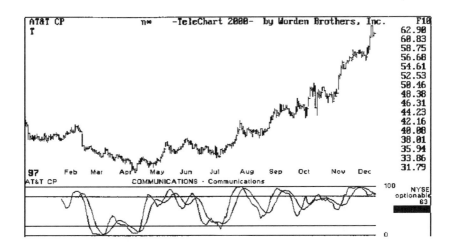

split 2:1 in December 1997, but traded above $20 for most of the year), I prefer to play these as rolling options, which we discuss in the next chapter.

RANGE RIDERS: CASE STUDIES

By studying the charts of several successful range riders and becoming familiar with their characteristics, you'll be in a better position to recognize them early and take advantage of their climb. I've included in this chapter six range riders, each of which emerged from a rolling pattern and went on to increases of over 100% during the course of the year.

The following case studies were selected not because they were so unusual or exceptional, but because they are *typical* of the way range riders behave and perform. By studying their behavior, you'll be better able to recognize their patterns and profit from them.

"Any man who is a bear on the future of this country will go broke."
—J. P. MORGAN

CASE STUDY #1 - MUSICLAND STORES

Musicland Stores (MLG) is the nation's number one specialty retailer of prerecorded home entertainment. They operate over 1,400 stores nationwide, including Musicland, Sam Goody, and Media Play. During 1995 and 1996 the stock price declined from over $10 to under $1. By early 1997 it was rolling in the $1 to $1.50 range.

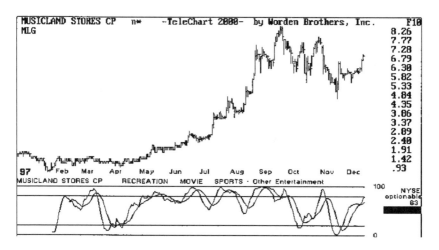

Starting in May, analysts' estimates of improving earnings started to move the stock price higher. While no positive earnings were reported, the losses had been trimmed. Revenues and number of stores were increasing. By third quarter 1997 MLG was trading above $8 per share, an increase of over 700% from earlier in the year. By year-end, the stock was rolling again, but in a $6 to $8 range. The company had no long-term debt and all that was required to lift the stock's price to a more favorable range was improved earnings and continued growth.

"Don't forget until too late that the business of life is not business, but living."

—B. C. FORBES

CASE STUDY #2 - INTERNATIONAL COMFORT PRODUCTS

International Comfort Products (ICP) is a Canadian manufacturer of heating and air conditioning products and steel pipes. Following four unprofitable years, their stock price had slid to a trading range under $1 by late 1995. It rolled briefly in that low range. Projections for 1996 indicated shareholders could expect a profit for the year. The stock immediately began its steady climb throughout all of 1996 and 1997, from under $1 to over $9 a share. During the last half of 1997, it was rolling nicely in the $7 to $9 range.

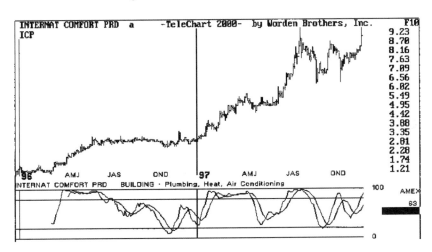

ICP provides another good example of how an unprofitable basic manufacturing company can have an 800% increase in the price of its stock with a relatively small earnings increase. There was no dramatic breakthrough, no merger or acquisition, no wildly successful new product. Just a subtle shift in the way they had been doing things all along.

"Do not anticipate trouble, or worry about what may never happen. Keep in the sunlight."

—BENJAMIN FRANKLIN

Case Study #3 - Anika Therapeutics

Anika Therapeutics (ANIK) is a range rider which began 1997 trading around $3.50 per share. They manufacture hyaluronic acid for use in surgical and other therapeutic applications.

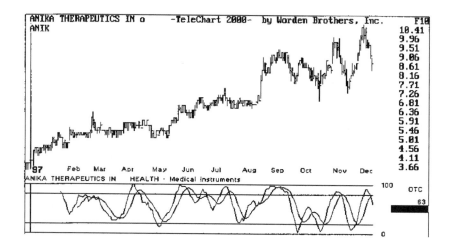

ANIK began the year with a new five-year contract with a major customer. The result was improved earnings (although still showing a net loss), and a stock price whose steady climb was punctuated by occasional dips. During the year the stock climbed from $3.50 to over $9 a share. By year-end it was rolling again in a $7 to $9 range.

"We must not measure greatness from the mansion down, but from the manager up."

—Jesse Jackson

CASE STUDY #4 - AMERICAN BINGO AND GAMING

American Bingo and Gaming (BNGO) operates bingo and video gaming centers, primarily in the southern U.S. They operated in 1994 and 1995 at a loss. By early 1996, expansion and increasing revenues moved them into the black. But their stock continued to roll in the $1 to $2 range. Even when they were turning in sustained earnings, investors had a hard time taking bingo seriously (there are virtually no institutional investors holding the stock).

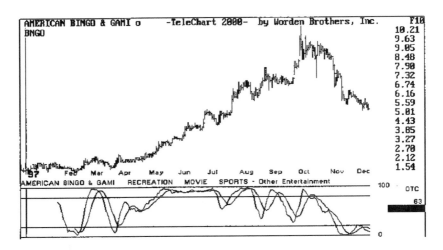

By mid 1997, investors finally saw some value in bingo as a business and sent the stock price up to the $8 range. By year-end BNGO appeared to be rolling again, but now in the more "respectable" $6 to $8 range.

"No one can possibly achieve real and lasting success or get rich in business by being a conformist."

—J. PAUL GETTY

CASE STUDY #5 - ULTRA PAC

Ultra Pac (UPAC) manufactures plastic containers used primarily for the food industry. These are the kind of disposable containers you put a muffin or hamburger in. The company's earnings tumbled in fiscal 1995-96. As a result, the stock price rolled in the $2 to $3 range for nearly a year.

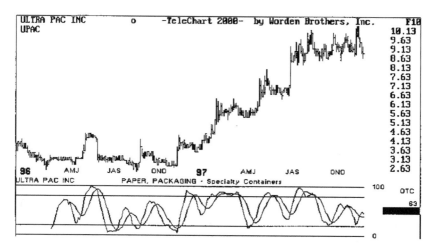

But the earnings for fiscal 1996-97 came back strongly, lifting the stock price to $10 per share. For most of the last half of 1997, UPAC was rolling steadily in the $8 to $10 range, unscathed by the mini-crash of October 1997.

"The adventure of getting your college money in cash now is that you can invest it in something with a higher return than a diploma."

—CAROLINE BIRD

CASE STUDY #6 - MEDIA ARTS GROUP

Media Arts Group (ARTS) manufactures and markets gifts, collectibles, and decorative accessories that are primarily the licensed works of co-owner Thomas Kincaid. Most of their goods are sold on the cable TV shopping channels such as QVC. This direct marketing approach has delivered consistent results.

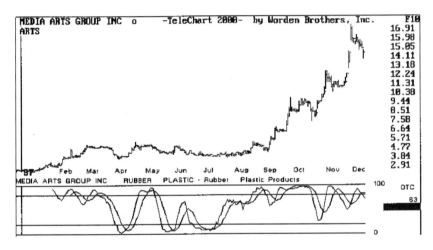

ARTS rolled in the $2 to $3 range for most of 1996 before it began its steady march upward. It closed 1997 at $15 a share. That's a healthy 500% increase for those who bought it as a Rolling Stock in early 1997.

"My idea of a group decision is to look in the mirror."
—WARREN BUFFETT

ADDING IT ALL UP

The preceding examples of range riders should paint a picture of a company involved in basic manufacturing or retail. They don't thrive on hype or glamour. They aren't creating a unique drug or developing cutting-edge, high-tech solutions. They are simply doing what they've always done, but doing it better.

I also observed that range riders are actually less likely to be held by large institutional investors. Unlike many high tech companies, which are primarily held by institutions, most of the range riders in our study had institutional ownership of less than 15%. This represents an opportunity for the typical small investor to be involved in a company before the big players arrive on the scene.

Are these range riders just Rolling Stocks that have become profitable? Not necessarily. Earnings seem to be the driving force, but sometimes it's just an undervalued, underrated company getting its day in the sun. Entire sectors can receive a lift as they come to the forefront of the news or experience a more favorable business climate. This can have a major upward push on a low priced Rolling Stock.

How do you find range riders like those profiled in the case studies? As with Rolling Stocks, these emerging range riders rarely appear on your stockbroker's radar screen. The best way to find them is by being an active trader in Rolling Stocks. In a way, this is your reward, or bonus, for patiently and faith-

---

"In an information society education is no mere amenity; it is the prime tool for growing people and profits."

—JOHN NAISBITT

fully sticking with these low priced rollers. Occasionally some of these ugly ducklings turn into magnificent swans. But you won't be likely to find them if you're not actively rolling.

Range riders are found in all price ranges. Unlike Rolling Stocks, which tend to be more concentrated in the lower priced stocks, range riders appear to be fairly evenly dispersed throughout the price spectrum. However, they frequently emerge from a stock that has been rolling in a low price range, therefore, looking for potential range riders among Rolling Stocks is a great place to start.

I also look for increasing volume as an indicator of an emerging range rider. Rapidly advancing stock prices are nearly always accompanied by increasing volume. The range riders in our study typically saw average daily volume increases of 25 to 50% as they began their ascent.

ROPING RANGE RIDERS EARLY

If the most difficult aspect of Rolling Stocks is to find them early, then the most difficult aspect of range riders is to spot them as they are first breaking resistance. Remember, when we go looking for range riders, we generally look among active Rolling Stocks.

The difficulty arises because as a stock transforms from a Rolling Stock into a range rider, there is almost always a false sell signal. The Rolling Stock reaches the top of its historic range, all of the sell signals are in place, and the stock

---

"If you have to go through too much investigation, something is wrong."

—WARREN BUFFETT

makes a quick dip (as if it were going back into its descent). Then, defying the technical signals, it reverses its downward trend and starts its climb.

If I were to detail the formula for getting in on a range rider, it could be summarized in the following steps:

1. Rolling Stock hits historic sell level.

2. A false sell signal occurs.

3. Stock takes a brief dip (less than 5%).

4. Dip is reversed and stock begins to climb past sell level.

5. The above step is accompanied by good news (especially an earnings turnaround).

By using this formula you should be able to spot a Rolling Stock as it turns into a range rider. You may have already sold the stock, but that doesn't keep you from buying back in on step three. Again, after a small dip, watch for buy signals and some improving fundamentals.

The pattern of range riders is also consistent with previous observations about Rolling Stocks. That is, Rolling Stocks trade within a given range and then generally go up after they have finished rolling. Most of the range riders in our study rolled, moved up dramatically, then went on to roll some more.

Most of the range riding companies which had such spectacular increases in the price of their stock were not high tech

"If you can count your money, you don't have a billion dollars."
—J. PAUL GETTY

start-ups, or biopharmaceutical firms creating some new wonder drug. No, they were nuts and bolts, basic American manufacturers. They were retailers, childcare centers, or makers of plastic containers. They persisted doing what they knew how to do best, eventually grabbing the attention of Wall Street.

"Obstacles are those frightening things you see when you take your eyes off the goal."

—HANNAH MORE

10
ROLLING OPTIONS

Amid all the jargon of Wall Street, perhaps no term is as appropriately named as *options*. *Options* give you *options*. Options give you flexibility. They give you alternatives and various ways to protect and profit from your investment. They enable you to leverage your trading capital far beyond what you could normally do with long stock positions. Options also allow you to improve your odds of winning when you invest.

The focus of this chapter is rolling options, that is, applying the principles of Rolling Stocks to the options market. The options market operates similar to the stock market. The major difference is that unlike stocks, options expire. But by applying the principles you've already acquired in Rolling Stocks, particularly in identifying support and resistance, you will be able to profit from Rolling Stocks in *both* their rise and their fall.

You can also use your expertise in Rolling Stocks to expand into higher-priced stocks. Most of our focus on Rolling Stocks has been with lower-priced stocks. But with options, you can make money on the volatility and roll of higher-priced stocks for the same amount of investment you would make in a lower-priced stock. You can, in effect, move up to a "nicer neighborhood" and start profiting from the minor rolls in some well-known, highly-capitalized, blue chip companies.

"If the models are telling you to sell, sell, sell, but only buyers are out there, don't be a jerk. Buy!"

—WILLIAM SILBER

There are many ways to use options and a variety of option strategies. I actively trade options using numerous methods and strategies, including covered calls, selling puts, credit spreads, and debit spreads. But as you might guess, rolling options is my favorite option strategy. I favor it for the same reason I favor Rolling Stocks; I love its simplicity. Rolling options, like Rolling Stocks, are predictable, reliable, and repeatable.

You can get a great education and hands-on experience with options through many of the seminars offered by Cook University (a course catalog is included in Appendix III). Books such as *Wall Street Money Machine* and *Stock Market Miracles* by Wade Cook will also give you an excellent understanding of the various strategies for making money using options. My intent in this chapter is to give you an overview so that you will be able to recognize the options market as an additional means of profiting from the Rolling Stock strategy.

AN OPTIONS PRIMER

An option is a contract that gives the owner the right, but not the obligation, to buy or sell an underlying stock at a specified price on or before a specified date. Two types of options are available, calls and puts. Calls give the owner the right to *buy* stock at the specified price, while puts give the owner the right to *sell* stock at the specified price. When an investor buys a call, he is expecting the price of the underlying stock to go up. When he buys a put, he is expecting the price of the underlying stock to go down.

"Success is simply a matter of luck. As any failure."

—EARL WILSON

Options are a type of investment known as derivatives. Their value is derived from or linked to the underlying security. When you own an option, you do not necessarily own the stock. You do not receive dividends on the stock. An option is not a down payment on the stock. It is simply a contract to buy or sell the stock at some future date and for an agreed upon price. For this right, the owner (buyer) pays a premium.

If Intel were trading at $85 a share and you expected it to go up in the next two months, you could buy a contract to purchase 100 shares of Intel (INTC) in two months at $90 a share. The $90 price is called the "strike price." That is the price at which you could buy the stock if you were to exercise your option. You might pay a premium of $2 per share for that right. Since option contracts are issued in units of 100 shares, your $2 call option for the 100 shares would cost you $200 ($2 x 100 shares).

Although the purchase of an option gives you the right to exercise the option by buying or selling the underlying security, that is not why most people buy options. My intent in buying options is to sell the option at a profit before expiration.

The main reason for investing in options is embodied in this next sentence. It is a phrase and a principle taught by Wade Cook to students at Wall Street Workshops™ throughout the country: *When there is a small movement in the stock, there is a magnified movement in the option.* The following table illustrates this point:

"Courage is doing what you're afraid to do. There can be no courage unless you're scared."

—Eddie Rickenbacker

General Electric (GE)	Strike Price = $80
Stock Price	Option Price
$74	$0.50
$76	$1.00
78	$1.50
79	$2.00
80	$2.50
82	$3.00

As the GE stock price moves from $76 to $78 (a movement of only $2^1/_2$%) the value of the option increases from $1 to $1.50 (a movement of 50%). If you had purchased 10 contracts at $1 per share when the stock was at $76, your total cost would have been $1,000 (10 contracts x 100 shares per contract x $1) plus commissions. You now control a block of 1,000 shares of stock. If you had purchased the stock directly, 1,000 shares would have cost you $76,000. But by holding the option, you're leveraging your money and controlling a large amount of stock with a small amount of money.

When the stock price is above the strike price of a call option, it is said to be "in the money." When the price of the stock is below the strike price of a call option it is "out of the money." Going back to the GE example, if you were to purchase an option for the $80 strike price when the stock is at $82, your $3 option position would be "in the money." You have purchased the right to buy the stock at $80 and it is already at $82. This $2

"We go to the movies to be entertained, not to see rape, ransacking, pillage, and looting. We can get all that in the stock market."
—Kennedy Gammage

difference (the in the money portion) is called the "intrinsic value" of the option. The remaining $1 is referred to as "time value."

Options have risks different from those associated with stocks. The main difference is that options expire. Because they expire, a portion of their value (the time value) erodes over time, with its most dramatic drop occurring immediately prior to expiration. Because options are a leveraging vehicle, you can lose your entire investment if the price of underlying stock moves against you. As a result, many options expire worthless.

Because options are such a flexible form of investing, there are also ways to use options which are actually less risky than owning stock outright. Some option plays are very conservative strategies, used by the savviest investors. Options also allow you to parcel out your risk in bite-size chunks.

OPTION PLAYS WITH ROLLING STOCKS

While most Rolling Stocks are going to be found among the lower priced stocks, there are some highly profitable, successful, larger companies whose stocks also have a rolling pattern. Many of the higher-priced Rolling Stocks don't have as large a percentage roll as the lower priced stocks. For example, the following chart of Chrysler (C) shows a good roll in the $34 to $37 range. This is a roll of less than 9%, but it is repeatable, reliable, and predictable.

You could buy 1,000 shares of Chrysler stock for $34,000 with the expectation of selling it a month later for $37,000. In

---

"Markets are currently in a state of uncertainty and flux, and money is made by discounting the obvious and betting on the unexpected."
—GEORGE SOROS

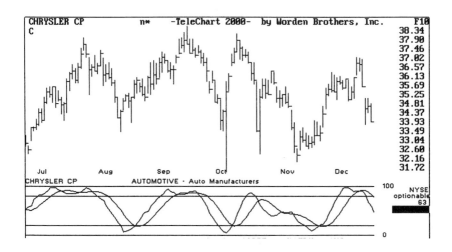

doing so you would put all $34,000 at risk and tie up those funds for the duration of the roll. But when the stock is at $34 you could also purchase the $35 call option for 75¢ or $750 for 10 contracts thereby controlling the same 1,000 shares. As the stock price advances to $37, your option is now in the money and worth $2.50 per share or $2,500.

Chrysler (C)	Strike Price = $35
Stock Price	Option Price
$34	$0.75
$35	$1.00
36	$1.75
37	$2.50

"The worst bankrupt in the world is a person who has lost his enthusiasm."

—H. W. ARNOLD

If you had invested in the stock, you would have tied up $34,000 for a 9% rate of return. By playing the option, you tie up $750 for a 200% return. When you invest in the stock, you have $34,000 at risk. Granted, it's unlikely the stock would ever plummet to zero in a month's time, but you still have that amount at risk. With the option, the maximum amount you can lose is your $750 premium.

Because of the leveraging power of options, I don't need to look for a 20 or 30% roll as I might be inclined to do with stock. Instead, I focus more on finding reliable small rolls. In looking for rolling option candidates, I still used the same buy signals, technical, and fundamental analysis I use when buying low priced Rolling Stocks. If anything, the selection process is easier because there is more information available for the larger, more widely traded high priced Rolling Stocks.

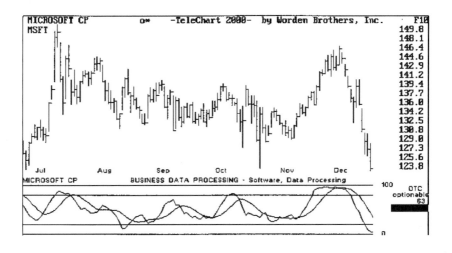

"Chance favors the informed mind."

—LOUIS PASTEUR

When I play rolling options, the price of the stock is of little consequence. Microsoft (MSFT) was rolling in a predictable $130 to $140 range for much of 1997. As a Rolling Stock it would only have yielded a return of around 7% on a fairly large amount of cash invested.

The option was likewise more expensive than most, because with a higher priced stock a larger dollar fluctuation could be expected. When the stock was trading at $130 you could buy an option with a strike price of $130 for the next month for $3.50. If you had purchased 10 contracts, your cost would have been $3,500. When the stock rolled up to $140, your options would now be worth over $10,000. It's hard not to get excited with a 185% one-month return on a relatively reliable roll such as this.

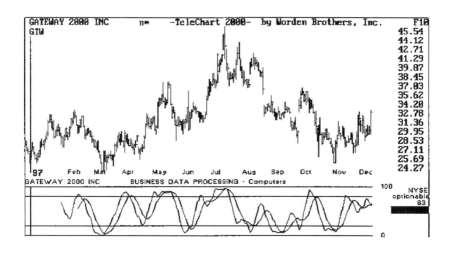

"Good judgement is usually the result of experience and experience is frequently the result of bad judgement."

—ROBERT LOVELL

Gateway 2000 (GTW), the #2 direct marketer of PCs, had a year marked by volatility. The stock's price had fluctuations of between 5 and 10% every month. Although this type of roll is hardly reliable, it certainly was repeatable. Like many options traders, I came to recognize the roll in the first half of the year, and profited repeatedly throughout the remainder of the year by buying call options on dips.

In 1997 the stock price of Pepsico, the #2 soft drink maker in the world and diversified food and drink company, increased over 35%. In addition, they spun off their largest division—Taco Bell, Pizza Hut, and KFC restaurant chains—to form TRICON Global Restaurants. But in spite of such consistent strength, the stock price had no fewer than 12 repeated dips of over 5%, each of which could have produced a phenomenal return on an option play.

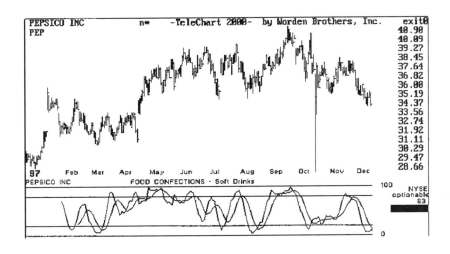

"A statistician is someone who can draw a straight line from an unwarranted assumption to a foregone conclusion."

—Anonymous

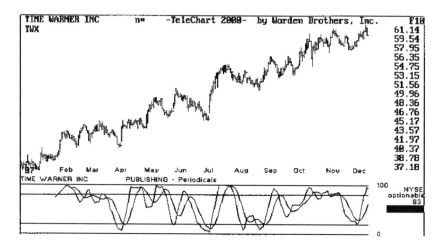

I never really seemed to think of Time-Warner (TWX) as a Rolling Stock. If anything, it was a strong range rider, trending solidly upward throughout most of 1997. Yet a month never passed without it experiencing a roll between 5 and 10%.

As a buyer of short term (one to three months from expiration) in-the-money call options, you could have made money every single month by simply buying on any dip of 5 to 10%. TWX is just one example of hundreds of upward trending stocks whose climb is barely broken by dips and short term pullbacks. These dips are ideal buying opportunities, especially for options traders.

STRATEGIES FOR SUCCESS

I view my rolling option plays as a conservative options strategy. I like to provide myself as much of a safety cushion as possible. With options that safety cushion comes in two forms,

"Successful investing is anticipating the anticipation of others."
—JOHN MAYNARD KEYNES

time and money. Practically speaking, you can give yourself these two safety cushions by following these two rules:

1. Give yourself at least twice as much time as you think you need to reach your target price. I give myself twice the time I think I need for two reasons. First, stocks don't always perform according to my timetable. I want the extra time so that if the stock makes an unexpected dip or delay in its climb, I will still have enough time to turn a profit. Secondly, most of the time value of an option is loaded into the month prior to expiration, and the steepest decline in the time value occurs in the month prior to expiration. I don't want the time value of my option to be declining as fast as my stock price or intrinsic value is increasing. I would prefer to pay a relatively small amount for additional time, and sell the option (and the more expensive last month time value) at least a month prior to expiration.

2. Buy slightly in-the-money options. I buy slightly in-the-money options because they provide the greatest safety. While the potential returns may not be as spectacular, I find that on rolling options, the in-the-money play is more consistently profitable.

OPTIONS - A SMART MARKET

In many ways, the options market is smarter than the stock market. The historic and implied volatility of a stock is an important element in the pricing of the option. When market makers price options, they take into account the subtle inefficiencies of the market and the ways the market responds to news.

"The American opportunity of ours gives everyone a great opportunity if we only seize it with both hands."

—AL CAPONE

When a stock has a predictable rolling pattern, the options market builds that expected roll into the price of the option. The result is an option that may be overpriced. As the price of the stock increases, the accompanying option price will increase more slowly. You may still be able to make a good profit on the option, but the odds may have been stacked against you.

One method of testing the degree to which option market makers have overvalued or "fluffed up" an option is to compare the ask price of the option to a theoretical value of the option. This theoretical value is calculated based on a model developed in 1973 by professors Fisher Black and Myron Scholes. Their work in options valuation earned them the Nobel Prize for Economics in 1997. Most brokers can tell you what the Black-Scholes valuation is on any listed option. Some online brokers also offer this comparison. By comparing that theoretical valuation with the actual option ask price, you can get a better picture of how fairly valued or overpriced your option might be.

On the floor of the Chicago Board of Options Exchange (CBOE) are signs that read "no standing." I take that as advice for successful options trading. Options require action and quick movement. Standing still can be dangerous since time is constantly eroding the value of your option. As with a Popsicle on a hot summer day, you need to move fast if you want to enjoy it before it melts.

"The first rule is not to lose. The second rule is not to forget the first rule."

—Warren Buffett

11

ACCOUNT STRATEGY

By now I hope you've proven to yourself that Rolling Stocks have the kind of profit potential that would make any portfolio look good. They provide you with safe, reliable, predictable, and repeatable returns. They can be used in the smallest of accounts by those with relatively little experience, or they can be the star performer in an account built on more solid, blue chip stocks.

Where do Rolling Stocks fit in a risk/reward spectrum? I hope that is a question you ask yourself regarding every investment. You should understand that every investment has a level of risk associated with it. Every investment also has an expected return. Once those two factors have been quantified, you can then make some approximation as to what the associated risk/reward ratio is.

```
High │            Buying Calls & Puts
     │        Selling Puts
REWARD│ Rolling Stock
     │ Covered Calls
     │
 Low └──────────────────────────────
       Low                      High
                  RISK
```

"It's easier to graduate than to learn."

—ROBERT HALF

As an instructor for Wade Cook's Wall Street Workshop™, I have the opportunity to teach stock market strategies to investors with various levels of experience. Many come to the workshop with million dollar portfolios and years of experience trading options. Others come with a $2,000 account opened the week prior to the workshop. Some will be making the first stock market play of their lives during the Wall Street Workshop™.

As I teach 11 key strategies for generating cash flow and building a solid portfolio, I consistently advise students at all levels of expertise to learn any strategy by doing it first on paper. In addition to live trades, paper trades or "simutrades" are used throughout the workshop. Learning and mastering a strategy on paper is a safe and effective way to build a track record of success without putting any trading capital at risk.

Once students have learned all 11 strategies, I still advise them to start with the more conservative, reliable strategies. For well over 90% of the Wall Street Workshop™ students, I recommend Rolling Stocks and writing covered calls as safe, profitable starter strategies.

Choosing A Broker

With over 40 million brokerage accounts open in the U.S. today, there are thousands of brokers competing for the privilege of holding your money and executing your transactions. While the lines of distinction between full-service, discount, and online computer trading brokers have blurred in recent years, those three categories still provide us with a frame-

"We make a living by what we get, but we make a life by what we give."

—Winston Churchill

work and starting point to help you determine where you will get the best value.

FULL-SERVICE BROKERS

Until about 25 years ago, this was the only alternative available to most investors. Full-service brokerages like Merrill Lynch, Salomon Smith Barney, Morgan Stanley Dean Witter, Dain Rauscher, Piper Jaffray, and others provide reports, recommendations, and analysis on a wide variety of securities. They are also market makers and hold seats on the major stock exchanges. Brokers within these firms manage their own client base and their earnings and advancement within the brokerage is linked to the size, volume, and transactions generated by that client base.

The commissions charged by full-service brokers vary by number of shares and share price. I sampled several full-service brokers and found that on a transaction of 1,000 shares at $2 a share, the typical commission is $120. A typical commission for 1,000 shares at $5 a share is $145.

Discounting of commissions by full-service brokers is to be expected. Discounts typically range from 25 to 50% off the published commission rates. You need to negotiate your commission discount as you open your account. Naturally, the amount of your discount will be determined by the broker based on what the brokerage permits, the size of your account, and the expected number of transactions.

"If I had my life to live over again, I'd make the same mistakes, only sooner."

—TALLULAH BANKHEAD

Discount Brokers

Charles Schwab led the way in the discount brokerage business and many others have followed. While discount brokers may position themselves as "full-service discount brokers," "deep discount brokers," or make other distinctions, their basic approach is the same: to undercut full-service broker commissions by not providing costly research and analysis. The discount broker exists primarily to execute the transaction. Discount brokers will not call you with recommendations and are typically not market makers.

On a purchase of 1,000 shares at $2 a share, the typical discount broker will charge you $64 in commissions. The commission on 1,000 shares at $5 a share is $89. Most discount brokers will also offer additional discounts for trading via an automated telephone transaction.

Online Brokers

The Internet has become the means for millions of investors to obtain quotes, news, analysis and a full range of investment information. The number of online brokers has mushroomed in the past few years. By the end of 1997 there were an estimated three million online accounts in the U.S.

The competition among online brokers for their piece of the market is fierce. Commission rates have fallen dramatically from a flat $30 per trade on the high end to some that offer a flat rate under $10. Some online brokers are offering incentives such as your "first five trades are free" as an inducement to get your account.

"Victory goes to the player who makes the second to last mistake."
—Savielly Grigorievitch Tartakower

The chairman of a major online brokerage recently stated that he could foresee the time when, for a customer with a certain size margin account, there would be no commission. In fact, they might even pay the customer, on a per trade basis, to bring the account to them.

Clearly, the advent of online trading will continue to have a major impact on the how full-service and discount brokers offer and price their services. It's not surprising that the leading discount broker, Charles Schwab, is also the leading online broker, based on number of accounts. Already we have seen several full service brokers entering the online market as a means of keeping and attracting customers.

In comparing the benefits and services of each type of broker, I find that ultimately the decision comes down to value. I feel that on many trades, particularly in options, I receive better value and an ability to "get in the spread" with a full-service broker. The quality of execution, combined with advice and analysis, gives me better value.

That value becomes less evident on Rolling Stocks. When I'm making the selection, pinpointing the entry price, and making my GTC for the exit, I have had consistently superior trade execution with online brokers.

Trading On Margin

A brokerage account, which has been approved for buying stocks on margin, permits you to buy stock in excess of the cash balance in your account. The brokerage is lending you

"Don't be scared to take big steps—you can't cross a chasm in two small jumps."

—David Lloyd George

money and charging you interest to buy those securities on margin. The collateral for that loan is the value of the securities in your account.

In order to protect their loan, and to comply with regulatory requirements, certain stocks are not marginable. Typically those securities under $5 per share cannot be margined. Since many, if not most, of the stocks identified as Rolling Stocks are under $5, you will not be able to margin those stocks. If you want to use your margin ability to its fullest potential you may want to consider trading non-marginable, low-priced Rolling Stocks in an account better suited to that type of investment.

Many investors with experience and a track record of success in Rolling Stocks find an Individual Retirement Account (IRA) to be the best place to manage their Rolling Stock portfolio. An IRA has some unique advantages. Let's take a look:

Hidden Clues From Congress

An Individual Retirement Account (IRA) is a personal pension plan that provides you both the benefits of a tax deduction *and* a tax shelter. If you qualify, an IRA is easily administered and highly advantageous tax reduction and investment strategy. I only wish it was available to more people and permitted higher levels of contribution. If you qualify for an IRA and don't take advantage, you are missing out on one of the best free rides that Congress gives.

But wait just a minute, Congress isn't in the habit of giving free rides to Americans who work and invest. Could there

---

"When you reach for the stars, you may not get one, but you won't come up with a handful of mud either."

—Leo Burnett

be another motive here? I believe Congress was sending a clue to the American taxpayer. The hidden message is this: "You had better start doing some serious retirement investing on your own, because the plan we set up for you (Social Security) is deplorable; and, by the way, it may not be there when you retire."

One national leader has pointed out that more people under the age of 30 believe in UFOs than believe that their Social Security pensions will be waiting for them when they retire. Everyone, particularly those young enough to plan ahead for a great retirement need to take specific action to ensure that their wealth accumulation and asset protection is secure. This has always been, and will always be an *individual* responsibility.

With that message in mind, you need to learn all you can about financing a great retirement. Let's start with an IRA. An IRA has two significant benefits:

Benefit 1: Contributions to an IRA are deductible from your gross income for federal income tax purposes. This benefit is available whether or not you itemize deductions on your federal tax form.

Benefit 2: IRA earnings (the capital gains generated from the sale of your stock) are tax deferred for the life of the account and are taxed only at withdrawal.

With the new Roth IRAs, the contributions are not deductible from taxable income. However, qualified withdrawals are

"Man's mind, once stretched by a new idea, never regains its original dimensions."

—OLIVER WENDELL HOLMES

tax free. So, you pay taxes on the seed rather than on the harvest. All earnings build up tax free, and are withdrawn tax free.

WHO BENEFITS FROM AN IRA?

The greatest beneficiaries are those who need it most, working people not covered by an employer's pension or retirement plan. If you fall into that category (nearly half of all Americans do), then an IRA is one of the best investment platforms you can find. Your contributions are fully deductible from your gross income.

If you participate in an employer-sponsored retirement plan, you now may also be able to establish a deductible IRA. Prior to 1998, if you or your spouse participated in an employer-sponsored retirement plan, you could not set up a tax-deductible IRA if your adjusted gross income was over $35,000 (single) or $50,000 (married filing jointly). Beginning in 1998, however, these adjusted gross income limits will rise until the year 2007, when the limit will reach $60,000 (single) or $100,000 (married filing jointly).

As always, Congress has put an irritating condition on this deductibility. If you are married and are *not* participating in an employer's pension or retirement plan, but your spouse *is*, then it's guilt by association. As far as the government is concerned, you are not permitted to deduct your IRA contributions if your combined adjusted gross income is over the limit.

Even though the tax deductibility of IRA contributions is not available to everyone, the tax-deferred benefit is. That

"You want 21% risk free? Pay off your credit cards."
—ANDREW TOBIAS

is, the earnings from the sale of stock that would normally be considered a capital gain will not be taxed until the money is withdrawn.

INVESTING IN AN IRA

With the benefits of tax deductibility and tax deferral, everyone who qualifies should have an IRA. But with these benefits come some limitations to the kind of investment strategies that can be used in an IRA.

For all practical purposes, you cannot buy securities on margin within an IRA account. Aside from the accounting nightmare, it is possible that a large drop in the price of a margined stock could result in a margin call. A margin call could force you to contribute an amount in excess of the allowable annual contribution.

For the same reason, equity options cannot be purchased within an IRA. Even though most people buy options with the intent of selling the option prior to expiration, should you choose to exercise your option, a contribution in excess of the allowable maximum could be required.

Another reason you are not permitted to trade options within an IRA is that options expire. Therefore, they are inherently more risky than owning stock. Even though trading options can be very profitable, the government does not want to permit people to place their retirement plan in such a risky investment.

"If you don't profit from your mistakes, someone else will."
—YALE HIRSCH

The exception to the above limitation on options is that you are permitted to write covered calls within an IRA. In this case you would be writing (selling) a call option on stock you already own. The premium on the sale of the call is credited directly to your IRA. Writing covered calls is a safe and profitable investment strategy that every investor should become familiar with. Through the Wall Street Workshop™, Cook University, and audio/video tape series, Wade Cook Seminars provides an excellent education in covered calls, options, and other investment strategies.

Any brokerage can set up a self-directed IRA that will allow you to buy and sell stock within a brokerage account designated as an IRA. This account can be through a full-service brokerage, a discount broker, or in an online computer trading account.

Where I Roll And Why

My vehicle of choice for trading Rolling Stocks is a self-directed IRA through an online computer trading account. In fact, my IRA is made up almost exclusively of Rolling Stocks. While I have several accounts with both full-service brokers and with online computer trading brokerages, I trade Rolling Stocks only in my online IRA account.

I enjoy working with full-service brokers and value the advice and quality execution on trades. Nearly all of my options trades are with full-service brokers. I have found that on time-sensitive, highly-leveraged plays such as options, I receive excellent execution from full-service brokers. I feel, and I know

"Don't gamble! Take all your savings and buy some stock and hold it till it goes up, then sell it. If it doesn't go up, don't buy it."
—Will Rogers

of other traders who have quantified this, that the quality of execution offered by a good full-service broker can more than pay the commission difference.

However, my experience has also been that there are very few brokers who have studied and developed a Rolling Stock strategy. Very few brokers actually track and monitor Rolling Stocks in a systematic manner. When most brokers look at the chart of a Rolling Stock, all they see is a low priced stock trading in the same range for several months. They usually don't get very excited about that.

Since I find most of my Rolling Stocks through my own research or on W.I.N.™, I don't feel the need for the broker's recommendation. Furthermore, once I've found a stock with a rolling pattern, I do most of my own fundamental and technical analysis. When it comes to Rolling Stocks, I do my own homework and make my own decisions. I use a broker strictly for execution.

Since most of the Rolling Stocks I invest in are in the $5 and under range, I find they are neither optionable nor marginable. It makes sense, therefore, to trade these stocks in my only account that prohibits options and margin trading—*my IRA!*

But even in a self-directed IRA brokerage account, I have the choice of setting up the account with a full-service broker, a discount broker, or an online computer trading brokerage. The full-service brokers I work with are not market makers in the

"Do not argue with the market, for it is like the weather: though not always kind, it is always right."

—KENNETH WALDEN

low priced Rolling Stocks I invest in, so they typically are in no better position to secure a more favorable, in-the-spread price. I have found that by placing a limit day order with an online brokerage, I am just as likely to be filled as if I had placed the same order with a full service broker.

Another compelling reason to trade Rolling Stocks online is value. I like to take advantage of retail discounts. I regularly look for "loss leaders," that is, discounts offered by retailers that are often at or below cost as an inducement to get your loyalty and more profitable business.

Clearly, an online trade with a commission under $10 is not a highly profitable transaction for an online brokerage. What they really want is your more profitable margin account and options business. Unlike full-service brokers, whose options commissions are typically less than a similar stock transaction, online brokers often charge two or three times more for an options trade. Likewise, margin interest rates in online brokerages are often higher than those offered by full-service brokers.

Naturally the commission savings with the online broker can be substantial, but that is not my primary consideration. Broker's commissions are an expected and relatively minor cost of doing business in the stock market. However, all other factors being equal, I'll take the lower commissions.

"You don't need to be a rocket scientist. Investing is not a game where the guy with the 160 IQ beats the guy with 130 IQ."
—WARREN BUFFETT

12

SAMPLE RETURNS

I don't want anyone to come to the end of this book thinking that you have to be some kind of psychic phenomenon or super hero to make great returns in the stock market. Success in Rolling Stocks takes some discipline, specialized knowledge, and a basic set of tools such as a phone and a home computer. Once you have these things in place, *anyone* can achieve results that will put you on the wealth track.

The charts and tables of sample returns in this chapter will expand your idea of what a Rolling Stock is. It will enable you to use the rolls common to all stocks to generate powerful returns, and to do it *again, and again, and again.* These kinds of profits can turn *any* brokerage account into a million dollar portfolio *in no more than 3¹/₂ years.*

I can make that claim because it's true. The power of compounding can take any account with as little as $500 (most of you will start with far more than that) and, by generating returns of 20% a month, create a million dollar portfolio in just 42 months (that's 3¹/₂ years)! Furthermore, if you do this all in an IRA, the gains on your million dollar portfolio will be tax deferred.

Here are sample returns to show you the kinds of simple, predictable steps that build a million dollar account:

"Refrain from covetousness, and thy estate shall prosper."
—PLATO

THE ALPHA MICROSYSTEMS POP FLY PLAY

I had been rolling Alpha Microsystems (ALMI) for some time, but even I wasn't expecting the spike it made in one day's trading.

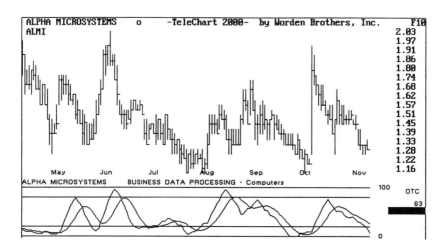

Oct 8	Bought	1,000 shares	@	$1.25 =	$1,250
Oct 14	Sold	1,000 shares	@	$1.75 =	$1,750
	Total Profit				**$500**
	Rate of Return (6 days)				**40%**

"Even if you're on the right track, you'll get run over if you just sit there."

—WILL ROGERS

INSIDE THE PARK HOME RUN BY 7TH LEVEL

On most Rolling Stocks, I'm looking for the repeatable 20 to 25% return. So when an opportunity comes along to double my money on each roll, I approach it with caution. The rolling pattern on the chart of 7th Level (SEVL) looks like some sort of thrill ride.

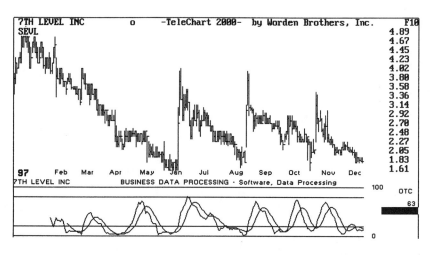

Oct 30 Bought 1,000 shares @ $1.75 = $1,750
Nov 5 Sold 1,000 shares @ $3.00 = $3,000
Total Profit **$1,250**
Rate of Return (6 days) **71%**

The above buy of SEVL was done on the weakest of technical buy signals, but more on the strength of the support level. Using that same support strength, I bought in again at $1.50 at year-end 1997.

"A wise man turns chance into good fortune."

—THOMAS FULLER

DURAMED STRIKES OUT, THEN SCORES WITH BIG HITS

I had played Duramed Pharmaceutical (DRMD) with some very profitable covered calls early in 1997. By mid year the stock had dropped from the $10 range to under $5 after the FDA rejected a drug they had been developing. Sure enough, after the big drop, it started an exciting and profitable rolling pattern. The buy shown here, as well as other successful rolls with DRMD were all made on clear stochastic buy signals.

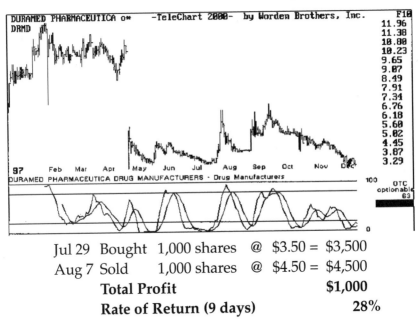

Jul 29	Bought	1,000 shares	@	$3.50 =	$3,500
Aug 7	Sold	1,000 shares	@	$4.50 =	$4,500
	Total Profit				**$1,000**
	Rate of Return (9 days)				**28%**

After I sold Duramed at $4.50, the stock went as high as $6.63 within a few days. There were no regrets on my part (well, maybe a little). I had achieved my return. The stock then moved fairly quickly back into a buy range.

"The knowledge of the world is only to be acquired in the world, and not in a closet."

—LORD CHESTERFIELD

The Fonar Double Play

Fonar Corporation (FONR) was rolling in the $2.50 to $3 range early in 1997. By having a GTC in place for the sale, I was able to score a "double play" and roll this twice in a single month.

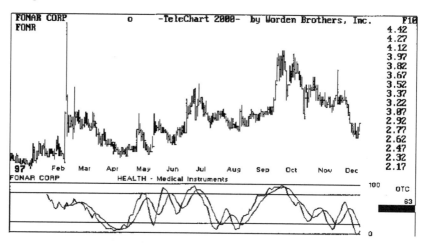

May 6	Bought	1,000 shares	@	$2.47 =	$2,473
May 12	Sold	1,000 shares	@	$3.00 =	$3,000
	Profit				**$527**
May 19	Bought	1,000 shares	@	$2.50 =	$2,500
May 29	Sold	1,000 shares	@	$2.94 =	$2,938
	Profit				**$438**
	Combined Profit				**$965**
	Rate of Return (23 days)				**38.6%**

"There is nothing more to be esteemed than a manly firmness and decision of character."

—William Hazlitt

THE IOMEGA-BUCKS ROLLING OPTION

For the past year Iomega (IOM) has been my favorite stock for rolling options. One look at the chart will tell you why. I was able to make these kinds of profits with Iomega monthly throughout most of the year. This is an option play, so you couldn't have done this in an IRA, however in addition to the transaction shown, I also played Iomega as a covered call, which is allowed in my IRA (or anyone else's, for that matter). *(Note: IOM split 2:1 in December 1997.)*

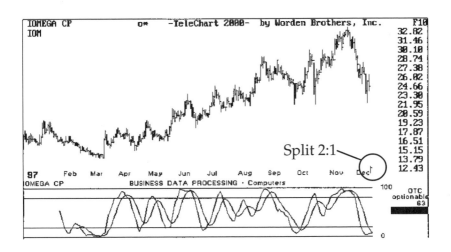

May 27	Bought	20 IOM June 17¹/₂ Call @ $.625 =	$ 625
June 5	Sold	20 IOM June 17¹/₂ Call @ $3.75 =	$3,750
	Total Profit		**$3,125**
	Rate of Return (9 days)		**500%**

"Riches are for spending, and spending for honor and good actions."
—FRANCIS BACON

Obviously, the sample returns you have just reviewed are phenomenal returns. But they are not necessarily uncommon or unusual. As you actively apply the Rolling Stock strategy, you will experience these kinds of returns in both stock and option plays.

As is always the case with the stock market, there will be more deals out there than you can possibly take advantage of. Your time and money will run out before the available attractive deals dry up. The question you need to ask as you make any stock or option play is, "What else can I do with my time and money?"

"He only is exempt from failures who makes no efforts."
—RICHARD WHATELY

13
PATTERNS FOR SUCCESS

Throughout this book we've focused on patterns for success. Success *always* seems to be found in patterns. In fact, I've never seen *random* success. No one drifts into success. Success in investing occurs when consistent patterns are understood and followed.

You've learned the strategies, methods, formulas, and rules for making money with Rolling Stocks, range riders, and rolling options. But knowing these patterns will be of little use unless they are applied in a systematic program of disciplined investing. You need to have a plan.

Here then, are six essential steps that will breathe life into your plan and enable you to generate cash flow and create wealth:

1. BECOME A STUDENT OF THE MARKETS

The Rolling Stock strategy is powerful, *predictably powerful*. Learn it inside and out, backwards and forward. Practice it continually and teach it to others. Always keep your eyes peeled for potential rollers. Ask friends or associates who are active in the market if they are aware of any Rolling Stocks. By doing this, you'll develop a network of "scouts" with whom you can share ideas.

"To become successful you must be a person of action. Merely to 'know' is not sufficient. It is necessary both to know and do."
—NAPOLEON HILL

Then expand beyond Rolling Stocks. Learn other cash flow strategies and investment strategies. Read everything you can get your hands on about the stock market. Subscribe to publications that focus on the market, such as *The Wall Street Journal* and *Forbes* (There are many others—I just happened to mention my two favorites.) These and other current periodicals will keep you tuned in to the market and abreast of current and long-term trends. They will also give you a variety of opinions from which you can form your own.

Take seminars and courses to keep your knowledge alive and fresh (a course catalog for Cook University is included in Appendix III). These opportunities for gaining specialized knowledge will be the best investment you can make. You'll make more because you know more. Acquired knowledge keeps paying off in ways you can never measure.

The learning process is continual. I'm reminded of a story told about Albert Einstein. At the age of 75 he was the guest of honor at a dinner. Seated next to him was a young college student. She turned to him and said, "Mr. Einstein, what is it you do?" Albert Einstein answered: "I am engaged in the study of physics." To which she responded, "Oh, physics. I studied that last year."

Albert Einstein, the most renowned scientific mind of our time described himself not as an accomplished physicist, but as a student, *engaged in the study* of physics. We would all be well served to take that as our approach, to be *engaged in the*

"It seems half the successful people I talk to stumbled into it or did it by accident."

—WADE B. COOK

study of the stock market. It is a boundless study, one which I have always found to be enjoyable, exciting, and rewarding.

2. DISCIPLINE YOURSELF

Successful investing has always been a discipline. Discipline is required at every point in the process. It takes discipline to save and commit funds to invest. It takes discipline to do the research required to make the right investment decisions. It takes discipline to learn the strategies correctly. It takes discipline to carefully manage your investments. It takes discipline to sell your investments in a timely and profitable manner.

Make at least one trade every day. These can be simutrades or real trades. In terms of developing discipline, it makes no difference whether your trade is made on paper or in a brokerage account. Monitor your positions daily and record your trades faithfully. As you close positions, study your successes and come to understand your failures.

Within a short time you'll find that just one or two simutrades a day won't be sufficient to fuel your account's cash flow appetite. As you practice and perfect the strategy, you'll see the profit potential from Rolling Stocks, and won't want to suffer the cost of lost opportunity.

3. STUDY SUCCESS

You are a product of your thoughts. Just as importantly, you have absolute power to feed thoughts to your subconscious mind. You can train your mind to be positive or nega-

"You can't get rich with a weather vane."

—WARREN BUFFETT

157

tive. You can train yourself to be a success or a failure. You have absolute control.

You can choose to feed your mind a diet of success-rich thoughts which can *only* produce a mind poised for success. You can separate yourself from the negative and create your own environment of success. The person who has conditioned his mind to make success its dominating thought soon finds that success also becomes the dominating action. When this occurs, like-minded people and situations are inevitably attracted to you.

As you study success, not only will you want to put yourself in proximity to other successful people, but these success-minded people will seek you out. As you surround yourself with people who have minds poised for success, there is an undeniable economic and psychic outpouring that takes place. This outpouring will result in concrete ideas, the emotional energy to fuel your pursuits, and a mental discipline that will stimulate your creativity and productivity.

Surround yourself with the kind of people you want to emulate. If you want to make a million dollars a year in the stock market, identify and surround yourself with people who are doing just that. Study what they do and how they behave. Listen to what they say, and *do what they do.*

4. Develop Decisiveness

The stock market does not reward procrastination. True, patience can have its reward, but lack of decision leads to lack

---

"Success and happiness come from the proper application of knowledge."

—Wade B. Cook

of action, which results in failure. Decisiveness can be developed and action can become habitual. Your success in the stock market hinges on your ability to be proactive, not reactive. The "wait and see" approach will leave you sitting behind as a spectator of the market.

Successful people are not easily influenced by others. They seek out the expertise and information others may possess, but the decision comes from within. Just as you have conditioned your mind to be successful, you will also condition yourself to be decisive.

You will come to gather information quickly. In fact, the only reason you gather information is so that you can make a better decision. Unless your information is actively leading you to a decision, you risk falling into the trap of "analysis paralysis."

5. DIVERSIFY

Just as the most important factors in real estate are "location, location, and location," the three most important factors in investing are "diversification, diversification, and diversification." By diversifying, you protect yourself from severe loss in a sagging sector or a down market.

This means you don't put all your eggs in one basket. You don't cluster too many stocks in one sector. In options, don't have your positions all focused on one expiration date. And most importantly for readers of this book, *you don't put your entire portfolio in Rolling Stocks*. Instead, you develop a well bal-

"He that trusteth in his riches shall fall: but the righeous shall flourish as a branch."
—PROVERBS 11:28

anced portfolio of solid blue chip stocks, growth stocks, income stocks, and other income producing assets as determined by you and your financial advisors.

Remember, when investing in Rolling Stocks, you're playing the strategy, not the stock. You buy the stock so that you can sell the stock. The name of the game is cash flow. Don't ever fall in love with the stock and thus betray the strategy.

Adjust as necessary. Don't let a bad experience with one stock or one strategy make you afraid to ever play that stock or strategy again. There will be inevitable losses. Accept them, learn from them, and move on.

As important as diversification is in the stock market, it is even more important in life. Do not confuse your *self worth* with the value of your assets. If your balance sheet goes down, *you* still have value. If your balance sheet goes up, *your* intrinsic value remains the same. If you start caring too much about your balance sheet, your life may be out of balance.

6. REWARD YOURSELF

When you have successes in the market, take a portion of those successes to reward yourself. No one should work for free. You need to pay yourself for your successes. You can do this in a number of ways. When you meet a weekly or monthly goal, take your spouse out to dinner to celebrate. Buy yourself a book on the stock market. Attend an educational workshop to enhance your skills. Take a friend out to the ballpark. Make winning fun and success a joy.

"Great things are not done by impulse but by a series of small things brought together."

—VINCENT VAN GOGH

Your reward may not always be material in nature. You may choose to give yourself the joy and satisfaction that can only come from sharing with others. You could reward yourself by taking a day to give service at a local shelter. You could make a special gift or cash donation to your church. You could spend time with your family on a well-earned vacation. Make the stock market a source of satisfaction in your life and let it spill over into the lives of others.

You may have noticed these six steps really have very little to do with the stock market. They have everything to do with life. The Rolling Stock strategy is a proven means of generating cash flow and enhancing wealth. When you have more cash flow and greater wealth, then the choice is yours as to how you use it. What you do with those rewards can change your life as well as the lives of those who surround you.

If you close this book and never make a trade, then we've both failed. Commit yourself now to implement a plan of action. Don't delay! Make whatever step is necessary to make your desires become reality.

I learned very early in this business that the stock market wasn't the most important thing in my life. It wasn't even in the top five. The stock market was simply a *vehicle* to help me obtain and enjoy those things that were most important to me. The stock market is a *great ride*, and it's the best way I know to help me achieve the really important things in my life. The stock market and Rolling Stocks have all the potential to give to you the same kind of great ride they've given me.

"The man who succeeds is one who, early in life, clearly discerns his object, and towards that object habitually directs his powers."
—EDWARD GEORGE BULWER-LYTTON

APPENDIX I

W.I.N.™ OVERVIEW

In the past year, Wealth Information Network™ (or W.I.N.™, as it is called) has firmly established itself as the premier online information source for stock market investors. This subscription-only service gives users a direct pipeline to Wade Cook and Team Wall Street. Subscribers can look over Wade Cook's shoulder and do what he is doing by simply replicating his trades which are posted online. For those investors who would rather do their own deals and tailor Wade Cook's strategies to their own financial situation, W.I.N.™ also has the finest set of market tools available.

The Rolling Stock section of W.I.N.™ is particularly useful for its ability to directly impact the profit potential of even the beginning investor's accounts. In addition to the resources of Wade Cook, his Research and Trading Department, and Team Wall Street, W.I.N.™ has dedicated a full-time stock analyst to research Rolling Stocks in an ongoing effort to keep up with new and emerging Rolling Stocks as well as profiling timely buying opportunities. So that you can see for yourself what W.I.N.™ has to offer on Rolling Stocks I have secured permission from W.I.N.™ to include some samples of the types of advisories which have appeared on W.I.N.™ in recent weeks. Normally these are only available to paid subscribers. I have included these entries unedited and exactly as they appear on

W.I.N.™. Following each entry I have provided my follow-up analysis of the entry showing potential returns.

> *October 16, 1997-One of our Facilitators placed a GTC order to buy 2,000 shares of Repligen Corp. (RGEN) at $1^1/$_{32}$. The stock was trading around $1^3/$_{16}$. This play was based upon a Rolling Stock strategy.*

The stock (RGEN) traded at $1^1/_{32}$ that day. If you had put in a GTC order to sell your shares at $1^3/_{16}$, or a 15% profit, you would have been filled the next day. If you wanted to go for a 20% profit you could have put in a GTC to sell at $1^1/_4$. You would have had to wait 14 days when you could have sold it for 1.25 per share for a 20% return.

> *October 13, 1997 - On October 8th in our Seattle workshop we purchased 1,000 shares of Frontier Airlines (FRNT) at $2^{15}/$_{16}$ as a Rolling Stock play, because the stock looked to be trading between $3 to $4. The stock popped up to $3^1/$_2$ yesterday and today it has settled back to around $3^3/$_8$. The roll to $4 may still happen, but we decided to put this money to work elsewhere so we placed our order to sell all 1,000 shares at market.*

Smart move. And good timing, too! On this play you would have achieved a 14.8% rate of return in five days. After they sold, the stock immediately headed downward, well below its original purchase price. Here's another quick play:

Tuesday, October 7, 1997 - Good morning everyone! This is Team Wall Street reporting in from the Wall Street Workshop™ in Boise, ID. One of our facilitators placed an order to buy 1,000 shares of Integrated HealthCare Inc. (ITHC) at a day limit of $2³/₄. The stock was trading around $2⁷/₁₆ x $2³/₄. We have placed an order with the broker that once we get filled on the purchase he will put in a GTC order to sell at $3¹/₂. We are playing this basically as a Rolling Stock, but it also has some good news coming out on it. This month the company will roll out a software product that supposedly will help track medical cost fraud. You can check for news in the Research area of WIN.

Sure enough, the stock traded at 2³/₄ on that day. Fortunately, Team Wall Street was following the Rule #1: know your exit before you go in the entrance. They placed a GTC order to sell at 3¹/₂ that would have been executed the next day. They achieved a 27% rate of return in just 24 hours.

Keep in mind, W.I.N.™ entries are not recommendations. They simply allow you to tap into the skill and experience of Wade Cook and his staff. You can follow what they do, or you may choose to disregard their lead entirely. Throughout W.I.N.™ you'll find disclaimers and reminders such as these:

Remember, do your own homework! Doing your own homework includes such things as checking a stock chart, looking at the fundamental financial data on a company such as profits and amount of capital, check-

ing on any news about the company and checking with your financial professionals before investing in any stock or option.

W.I.N.™ also lists about 75 Rolling Stocks by price range (under $5, $5 to $10, $10 to $15, and $15 to $20). It lists the approximate rolling range. This makes it easy for the W.I.N.™ subscriber to find stocks in their price range and make a selection of one that appears to be a good buying opportunity.

When you conduct your stock research on W.I.N.™, you save time by not having to move back and forth between sites. It's all a relatively seamless research environment that includes everything from charts, to fundamental analysis, to summaries of analysts' recommendations, and stock and option quotes.

Since a W.I.N.™ trial enrollment is offered to Wall Street Workshop™ participants, there is a great opportunity to couple the workshop strategies with the tutorial quality of W.I.N.™ to develop sound trading habits and yield spectacular results.

APPENDIX II
TRACKING FORMS

ROLLING STOCK TRACKING SHEET

Ticker	Company	Buy Date	Price	Quantity	Total Out	GTC	Sell Date	Price	Total In	Gain/ Loss	%

ROLLING STOCK TRACKING SHEET

Ticker	Company	Buy Date	Price	Quantity	Total Out	GTC	Sell Date	Price	Total In	Gain/Loss	%

Appendix III

Available Resources

The following books, videos, and audiocassettes have been reviewed by the Wade Cook Seminars, Inc. or Lighthouse Publishing Group, Inc. staff and are suggested as reading and resource material for continuing education to help with your financial planning, and real estate and stock market investments. Because new ideas and techniques come along and laws change, we're always updating our catalog.

To order a copy of our current catalog, please write or call us at:

Wade Cook Seminars, Inc.
14675 Interurban Avenue South
Seattle, Washington 98168-4664
1-800-872-7411

Or, visit us on our websites at:
www.wadecook.com
www.lighthousebooks.com

Also, we would love to hear your comments on our products and services, as well as your testimonials on how these products have benefited you. We look forward to hearing from you!

AUDIOCASSETTES

13 Fantastic Income Formulas—A free cassette
By Wade B. Cook

Learn the 13 cash flow formulas, some of which are taught in the Wall Street Workshop™. Learn to double some of your money in $2^1/_2$ to 4 months.

Zero To Zillions
By Wade B. Cook

A four-album, 16 cassette, powerful audio workshop on Wall Street—understanding the stock market game, playing it successfully, and retiring rich. Learn 11 powerful investment strategies to avoid pitfalls and losses, catch "day-trippers," "bottom fish," write covered calls, to possibly double your money in one week on options on stock split companies. Wade "Meter Drop" Cook will teach you how to make fantastic annual returns in your account.

Power Of Nevada Corporations—A free cassette
By Wade B. Cook

Nevada Corporations have secrecy, privacy, minimal taxes, no reciprocity with the IRS, and protection for shareholders, officers, and directors. This is a powerful seminar.

Income Streams—A free cassette
By Wade B. Cook

Learn to buy and sell real estate the Wade Cook way. This informative cassette will instruct you in building and operating your own real estate money machine.

Money Machine I & II

By Wade B. Cook

Learn the benefits of buying, and more importantly, selling real estate. Now the system for creating and maintaining a real estate money machine is available in audiocassette form. Money Machine I & II teaches the step-by-step cash flow formulas that made Wade Cook and thousands like him millions of dollars.

Money Mysteries of the Millionaires—A free cassette

By Wade B. Cook

How to make money and keep it. This fantastic seminar shows you how to use Nevada Corporations, Living Trusts, Pension Plans, Charitable Remainder Trusts, and Family Limited Partnerships to protect your assets.

Unlimited Wealth Audio Set

By Wade B. Cook

Unlimited Wealth is the "University of Money-Making Ideas" home study course that helps you improve your money's personality. The heart and soul of this seminar is to make more money, pay fewer taxes, and keep more for your retirement and family. This cassette series contains the great ideas from *Wealth 101* on tape, so you can listen to them whenever you want.

Retirement Prosperity

By Wade B. Cook

Take that IRA money now sitting idle and invest it in ways that generate you bigger, better, and quicker returns. This four audiotape set walks you through a system of using a self directed IRA to create phenomenal profits, virtually tax free! This is one of the most complete systems for IRA investing ever created.

The Financial Fortress Home Study Course
By Wade B. Cook

This eight-part series is the last word in entity structuring. It goes far beyond mere financial planning or estate planning. It helps you structure your business and your affairs so that you can avoid the majority of taxes, retire rich, escape lawsuits, bequeath your assets to your heirs without government interference, and, in short-bomb proof your entire estate. There are six audio cassette seminars on tape, an entity structuring video, and a full kit of documents.

Paper Tigers and Paper Chase
By Wade B. Cook

Wade gives you a personal introduction to the art of buying and selling real estate. In this set of six cassettes, Wade shares his inside secrets to establishing a cash flow business with real estate investments. You will learn how to find discounted second mortgages, find second mortgage notes and make them better, as well as how you can get 40%-plus yields on your money. Learn the art of structuring your business to attract investors and bring in the income you desire through the use of family corporations, pension plans, and other legal entities. A manual is included.

When you buy Paper Tigers, you'll also receive Paper Chase for free. Paper Chase holds the most important tools you need to make deals happen. Wade created these powerful tapes as a handout tool you can lend to potential investors or home owners to help educate them about how this amazing cash flow system works for them. It explains how you'll negotiate a lower interest rate if they make a larger payment. You will use this incredible tool over and over again.

The Real Estate Cash Flow System
Presented by Wade B. Cook

This six-volume audiocassette set, originally sold separately, contains everything you'll ever need to begin investing in real estate immediately, do so successfully, handle all of the business aspects and retire sooner than you ever thought possible. Just look at all the tremendous information that can be yours.

BOOKS

Wall Street Money Machine
By Wade B. Cook

Appearing on the *New York Times* Business Best Sellers list for over one year, *Wall Street Money Machine* contains the best strategies for wealth enhancement and cash flow creation you'll find anywhere. Throughout this book, Wade Cook describes many of his favorite strategies for generating cash flow through the stock market: Rolling Stock, Proxy Investing, Covered Calls, and many more. It's a great introduction for creating wealth using the Wade Cook formulas.

Stock Market Miracles
By Wade B. Cook

The anxiously-awaited partner to *Wall Street Money Machine*, this book is proven to be just as invaluable. *Stock Market Miracles* improves on some of the strategies from *Wall Street Money Machine*, as well as introducing new and valuable twists on our old favorites. This is a must read for anyone interested in making serious money in the stock market.

Bear Market Baloney
By Wade B. Cook

A more timely book wouldn't be possible. Wade's predictions came true while the book was at press! Don't miss this insightful look into what makes bull and bear markets and how to make exponential returns in any market.

Sleeping Like A Baby
By John C. Hudelson

Perhaps the most predominant reason people don't invest in the stock market is fear. *Sleeping Like A Baby* removes the fear from investing and gives you the confidence and knowledge to invest wisely, safely, and profitably.

You'll learn how to build a high quality portfolio and plan for your future and let your investments follow. Begin to invest as early as possible, and use proper asset allocation and diversification to reduce risk.

The Secret Millionaire Guide To Nevada Corporations
By John V. Childers, Jr.

What does it mean to be a secret millionaire? In *The Secret Millionaire Guide to Nevada Corporations,* attorney John V. Childers, Jr. outlines exactly how you can use some of the secret, extraordinary business tactics used by many of today's super-wealthy to protect your assets from the ravages of lawsuits and other destroyers using Nevada Corporations. You'll understand why the state of Nevada has become the preferred jurisdiction for those desiring to establish corporations and how to utilize Nevada Corporations for your financial benefit.

Million Heirs
By John V. Childers, Jr.

In his reader-friendly style, attorney John V. Childers, Jr., explains how you can prepare your loved ones for when you pass away. He explains many details you need to take care of right away, before a death occurs, as well as strategies for your heirs to utilize. Don't leave your loved ones unprepared—get *Millions Heirs.*

Real Estate Money Machine
By Wade B. Cook

Wade's first bestselling book reveals the secrets of Wade Cook's own system-the system he used to earn his first million. This book teaches you how to make money regardless of the state of the economy. Wade's innovative concepts for investing in real estate not only avoids high interest rates, but avoids banks altogether.

How To Pick Up Foreclosures
By Wade B. Cook

Do you want to become an expert money maker in real estate? This book will show you how to buy real estate at 60¢ on the dollar or less. You'll learn to find the house before the auction and purchase it with no bank financing-the easy way to millions in real estate. The market for foreclosures is a tremendous place to learn and prosper. *How To Pick Up Foreclosures* takes Wade's methods from *Real Estate Money Machine* and super charges them by applying the fantastic principles to already-discounted properties.

Cook's Book On Creative Real Estate
By Wade B. Cook

Make your real estate buying experiences profitable and fun. *Cook's Book On Creative Real Estate* will show you how! You will learn suggestions for finding the right properties, buying them quickly, and profiting ever quicker.

Owner Financing
By Wade B. Cook

This is a short but invaluable booklet you can give to sellers who hesitate to sell you their property using the owner financing method. Let this pamphlet convince both you and them. The special report, *"Why Sellers Should Take Monthly Payments,"* is included for free!

Real Estate For Real People
By Wade B. Cook

A priceless, comprehensive overview of real estate investing, this book teaches you how to buy the right property for the right price, at the right time. Wade Cook explains all of the strategies you'll need, and gives you 20 reasons why you should start investing in real estate today. Learn how to retire rich with real estate, and have fun doing it.

101 Ways To Buy Real Estate Without Cash
By Wade B. Cook

Wade Cook has personally achieved success after success in real estate. *101 Ways To Buy Real Estate Without Cash* fills the gap left by other authors who have given all the ingredients but not the whole recipe for real estate investing. This is the book for the investor who wants innovative and practical methods for buying real estate with little or no money down.

Brilliant Deductions
By Wade B. Cook

Do you want to make the most of the money you earn? Do you want to have solid tax havens and ways to reduce the taxes you pay? This book is for you! Learn how to get rich in spite of the updated 1997 tax laws. See new tax credits, year-end maneuvers, and methods for transferring and controlling your entities. Learn to structure yourself and your family for tax savings and liability protection. Available in bookstores or call our toll free number: 1-800-872-7411.

Wealth 101
By Wade B. Cook

This incredible book brings you 101 strategies for wealth creation and protection that you can't afford to miss. Front to back, it is packed full of tips and tricks to supercharge your financial health. If you need to generate more cash flow, this book shows you how through several various avenues. If you are already wealthy, this is the book that will show you strategy upon strategy for decreasing your tax liability and increasing your peace of mind through liability protection.

Blueprints For Success, Volume 1
Contributors: Joel Black, JJ Childers, Wade Cook, Keven Hart, Debbie Losse, Tim Semingson, Dan Wagner, Dave Wagner, Steve Wirrick, Gregory Witt, and Rich Simmons.

Blueprints For Success, Volume 1 is a compilation of chapters on building your wealth through your business and making your business function successfully. The chapters cover: education and information gathering, choosing the best business for you from all the different types of business, and a variety of other skills necessary for becoming successful. Your business can't afford to miss out on these powerful insights!

A+
By Wade B. Cook

A+ is a collection of wisdom, thoughts, and principles of success which can help you make millions, even billions of dollars and live an A+ life. As you will see, Wade Cook consistently tries to live his life "in the second mile," to do more than asked, to be above normal.

If you want to live a successful life, you need great role models to follow. For years, Wade Cook's life has been a quest to find successful characteristics of his role models and implement them in his own life. In A+, Wade will encourage you to find and incorporate the most successful principles and characteristics of success in your life, too. Don't spend another day living less than an A+ life!

Business Buy The Bible
By Wade B. Cook

Inspired by the Creator, the Bible truly is the authority for running the business of life. Throughout Business Buy The Bible, you are provided with practical advice that helps you apply God's work to your life. You'll learn how you can apply God's words to saving, spending and investing, and how you can control debt instead of being controlled by it. You'll also learn how to use God's principles in your daily business activities and prosper.

Don't Set Goals
By Wade B. Cook'

Don't Set Goals will teach you to be a goal-getter, not just a goal-setter. You'll learn that achieving goals is the result of prioritizing and acting. *Don't Set Goals* shows you how taking action and "paying the price" is more important that simply making the decision to do something. Don't just set goals. Go out and get your goals, go where you want to go!

Wade Cook's Power Quotes, Volume 1

By Wade B. Cook

Wade Cook's Power Quotes, Volume 1 is chock full of exciting quotes that have motivated and inspired Mr. Cook. Wade Cook continually asks his students, "To whom are you listening?" He knows that is you get your advice and inspiration from successful people, you'll become successful yourself. He compiled *Wade Cook's Power Quotes, Volume 1* to provide you with a millionaire-on-call when you need advice.

Y2K Gold Rush

By Wade B. Cook

As we approach the end of the millennium, newspapers and television newscasters drone on about Y2K. Computers will read the year 2000 as 1900! The issue is a definite problem, but in Y2K Gold Rush, Wade Cook discounts the need for this hysteria. First, businesses and individuals alike have been preparing for this problem. Secondly, and more importantly, people are now buying gold to protect themselves against all types of potential problems.

This book is about how to invest in gold. By reading *Y2K Gold Rush*, you will understand the historical importance of gold. You will learn about the ownership of gold coins and gold stocks, and the benefits of both. You will see that adding gold to your investment portfolio will diversify your assets, safeguard you and your family against catastrophe, and add excitement and profits.

Living In Color
By Renae Knapp

Renae Knapp is the leading authority on the Blue Base/Yellow Base Color System and is recognized worldwide for her research and contribution to the study of color. Industries, universities, and men and women around the globe use Renae's tried and true—scientifically proven—system to achieve measurable results.

In Living In Color, Renae Knapp teaches you easy to understand methods which empower you to get more from your life by harnessing the power of color. In an engaging, straightforward way, Renae Knapp teaches the scientific BlueBase/Yellow Base Color System and how to achieve harmony and peace using color. You will develop a mastery of color harmony and an awareness of the amazing role color plays in every area of your life.

VIDEOS

Dynamic Dollars Video
By Wade B. Cook

Wade Cook's 90 minute introduction to the basics of his Wall Street formulas and strategies. In this presentation designed especially for video, Wade explains the meter drop philosophy, Rolling Stock, basics of Proxy Investing, and writing Covered Calls. Perfect for anyone looking for a little basic information.

The Wall Street Workshop™ Video Series
By Wade B. Cook

If you can't make it to the Wall Street Workshop™ soon, get a head start with these videos. Ten albums containing 11 hours of intense instruction on rolling stock, options on stock split companies, writing covered calls, and eight other tested and proven strategies designed to help you increase the value of your investments. By learning, reviewing, and implementing the strategies taught here, you will gain the knowledge and the confidence to take control of your investments, and get your money to work hard for you.

The Next Step Video Series
By Team Wall Street

The advanced version of the Wall Street Workshop™. Full of power-packed strategies from Wade Cook, this is not a duplicate of the Wall Street Workshop™, but a very important partner. The methods taught in this seminar will supercharge the strategies taught in the Wall Street Workshop™ and teach you even more ways to make more money!

In The Next Step, you'll learn how to find the stocks to fit the formulas through technical analysis, fundamentals, home trading tools, and more.

Build Perpetual Income (BPI)—A videocassette

Wade Cook Seminars, Inc. is proud to present *Build Perpetual Income*, the latest in our ever-expanding series of seminar home study courses. In this video, you will learn powerful real estate cash-flow generating techniques, such as:

- Power negotiating strategies
- Buying and selling mortgages
- Writing contracts
- Finding and buying discount properties
- Avoiding debt

CLASSES OFFERED

Cook University

People enroll in Cook University for a variety of reasons. Usually they are a little discontented with where they are-their job is not working, their business is not producing the kind of income they want, or they definitely see that they need more income to prepare for a better retirement. That's where Cook University comes in. As you try to live the American Dream, in the life-style you want, we stand by ready to assist you make the dream your reality.

The backbone of the one-year program is the Money Machine concept-as applied to your business, to stock investments, or to real estate. Although there are many, many other forms of investing in real estate, there are really only three that work: the Money Machine method, buying second mortgages, and lease options. Of these three, the Money Machine stands head and shoulders above the rest.

It is difficult to explain Cook University in only a few words. It is so unique, innovative and creative that it literally stands alone. But then, what would you expect from Wade Cook? Something common and ordinary? Never! Wade and his staff always go out of their way to provide you with useful, tried-and-true strategies that create real wealth.

We are embarking on an unprecedented voyage and want you to come along. If you choose to make this important decision in your life, you could also be invited to share your successes in a series of books called *Blueprints For Success, Volume 1* (more volumes to come). Yes, it takes commitment. Yes, it takes drive. Add to this the help you'll receive by our hand-trained experts and you will enhance your asset base and increase your bottom line.

We want to encourage a lot of people to get in the program right away. You could save thousands of dollars, if you don't delay. Call right away! Class sizes are limited so each student gets personal attention.

Perpetual monthly income is waiting. We'll teach you how to achieve it. We'll show you how to make it. We'll watch over you while you're making it happen. Thank you for your consideration. We hope to see you in the program right away.

Cook University is designed to be an integral part of your educational life. We encourage you to call and find out more about this life-changing program. The phone number is 1-800-872-7411. Ask for an enrollment director and begin your millionaire-training today!

If you want to be wealthy, this is the place to be.

The Wall Street Workshop™
Presented by Wade B. Cook and Team Wall Street

The Wall Street Workshop™ teaches you how to make incredible money in all markets. It teaches you the tried-and-true strategies that have made hundreds of people wealthy.

The Next Step Workshop
Presented by Wade B. Cook and Team Wall Street

An advanced Wall Street Workshop™ designed to help those ready to take their trading to the next level and treat it as a business. This seminar is open only to graduates of the Wall Street Workshop™.

The Youth Wall Street Workshop™
Presented by Team Wall Street

Wade Cook has made a personal commitment to empower the youth of today with desire and knowledge to be self sufficient. Now you, too, can make a personal commitment to your youth by sending them to the Youth Wall Street Workshop™ and start your own family dynasty in the process!

Our Youth Wall Street Workshop™ teaches the power and money making potential of the stock market strategies of the Wall Street Workshop™. The pace is geared to the students, with more time devoted to vocabulary, principles and concepts that may be new to them.

If you're considering the Wall Street Workshop™ for the first time, take advantage of our free Youth Wall Street Workshop™ promotion and bring a son, daughter, or grandchild with you (ages 13 to 18, student, living at home).

Financial Clinic
Presented by Wade Cook and Team Wall Street

People from all over are making money, lots of money, in the stock market using the proven bread and butter strategies taught by Wade Cook. Is trading in the stock market for you?

Please accept our invitation to come hear for yourself about the amazing money-making strategies we teach. Our Financial Clinic is designed to help you understand how you can learn these proven strategies we teach at our Wall Street Workshop™. Discover for yourself how they work and how you can use them in your life to get the things you want for you and your family. Come to this introductory event and see what we have to offer. Then make the decision for yourself.

S.O.A.R. (Supercharging Otherwise Average Returns)
Presented by Bob Eldridge

This one-day workshop begins by teaching you some basic strategies using a "hands-on" approach. You will be amazed at how easy it is to apply these strategies to the 30 Dow Jones Industrial Average stocks. Using these same strategies, Bob Eldridge was able to resign from his job with the FAA as an air traffic control specialist and begin speaking full-time after only a few months of trading!

The One-Minute Commute (Trading At Home)
Presented by Keven Hart

This one-day clinic will take you being a semi-active investor to trading on a daily basis, giving you the freedom to dictate your own schedule and move forward on your own predetermined timeline. Trade from your home and stay close to your family. This condensed training will get you where you want to go by helping you practice trading as a business, showing you which resources produce wealth through crucial and timely information, selecting appropriate strategies, qualifying your trades and helping you time both entries and exits.

The Day Trader
Presented by Mike Coval

The Day Trader will teach you how to locate and profit on a daily basis from charts, news, and trends. You will also learn how outside indicators can and will influence a market. Learn how to find the hottest stocks in the hottest sectors and find out a stock's movement before the market opens. With this action-packed workshop, you will have the opportunity to find fast-moving stocks profiting in just minutes. At the end of the day you can sit back and count your profits, then start tomorrow all over again!

Executive Retreat
Presented by Wade B. Cook and Team Wall Street

Created especially for the individuals already owning or planning to establish Nevada Corporations, the Executive Retreat is a unique opportunity for corporate executives to participate in workshops geared toward streamlining operations and maximizing efficiency and impact.

Wealth Institute
Presented by Wade B. Cook and Team Wall Street

This three day workshop defines the art of asset protection and entity planning. During these three days we will discuss, in depth and detail, the six domestic entities which will protect you from lawsuits, taxes, or other financial losses, and help you retire rich.

Real Estate Workshop
Presented by Wade B. Cook and Team Main Street

The Real Estate Workshop teaches you how to build perpetual income for life, without going to work. Some of the topics include buying and selling paper, finding discounted properties, generating long-term monthly cash flow, and controlling properties without owning them.

Real Estate Bootcamp
Presented by Wade B. Cook and Team Main Street

This three to four day Bootcamp is truly a roll-up-your-sleeves-and-do-the-deals event. You will be learning how to locate the bargains, negotiate strategies, and find wholesale properties (pre-foreclosures). You will also visit a title company, look at properties and learn some new and fun selling strategies.

Business Entity Skills Training (BEST)
Presented by Wade B. Cook and Team Wall Street

Learn about the six powerful entities you can use to protect your wealth and your family. Learn the secrets of asset protection, eliminate your fear of litigation, and minimize your taxes.

ASSORTED RESOURCES

Wealth Information Network™ (W.I.N.™)

This subscription Internet service provides you with the latest financial formulas and updated entity structuring strategies. New, timely information is entered Monday through Friday, sometimes four or five times a day. Wade Cook and his Team Wall Street staff write for W.I.N.™, giving you updates on their own current stock plays, companies who announced earnings, companies who announced stock splits, and the latest trends in the market.

W.I.N.™ is also divided into categories according to specific strategies and contains archives of all our trades so you can view our history. If you are just getting started in the stock market, this is a great way to follow people who are doubling their money every $2^1/_2$ to 4 months. If you are experienced already, it's the way to confirm your feelings and research with others who are generating wealth through the stock market.

IQ Pager™

This is a system which beeps you as events and announcements are made on Wall Street. With *IQ Pager™*, you'll receive information about events like major stock split announcements, earnings surprises, important mergers and acquisitions, judgements or court decisions involving big companies, important bankruptcy announcements, big winners and losers, and disasters. If you're getting your financial information from the evening news, you're getting it too late. The key to the stock market is timing. Especially when you're trading in options, you need up-to-the-minute (or second) information. You cannot afford to sit at a computer all day looking for news or wait for your broker to call. *IQ Pager*™ is the ideal partner to the Wealth Information Network™ (W.I.N.™).

The Incorporation Handbook
By Wade B. Cook

Incorporation made easy! This handbook tells you who, why, and, most importantly, how to incorporate. Included are samples of the forms you will use when you incorporate, as well as a step-by-step guide from the experts.

Legal Forms
By Wade B. Cook

This collection of pertinent forms contains numerous legal forms used in real estate transactions. These forms were selected by experienced investors, but are not intended to replace the advice of an attorney. However, they will provide essential forms for you to follow in your personal investing.

Record Keeping System
By Wade B. Cook

A complete record keeping system for organizing all of the information on each of your properties. This system keeps track of everything from insurance policies to equity growth.

You will know at a glance exactly where you stand with your investment properties and you will sleep better at night.

Travel Agent Information
By John Childers and Wade Cook

The only sensible solution for the frequent traveller. This kit includes all of the information and training you need to be an outside travel agent for a stable company. There are no hassles, no requirements, no forms or restrictions, just all the benefits of travelling for substantially less every time.

EXPLANATIONS Newsletter

In the wild and crazy stock market game, *EXPLANATIONS* Newsletter will keep you on your toes! Every month you'll receive coaching, instruction, and encouragement with engaging articles designed to bring your trading skills to a higher level. Learn new twists on Wade's 11 basic strategies, find out about beneficial research tools, read reviews on the latest investment products and services, and get detailed answers to your trading questions. With *EXPLANATIONS*, you'll learn to be your own best asset in the stock market game and stay on track to a rapidly growing portfolio! Continue your education as an investor and subscribe today!

GLOSSARY

TECHNICAL TERMS

Ask – The current price for which a security may be bought (purchased).

At-the-close – The last price a security trades for, when the market stops trading for the day.

At-the-open – The price a stock security trades for, when the market starts trading for the day.

Balance of Power™ – A technical indicator developed by Worden Brothers which is designed to show patterns of systematic buying and selling by informed buyers.

Bid – The current price at which you could sell your security.

Buying a hedge – The purchase of future options, or other investments, as a means of protecting against an increase or decrease in the price of a security in the future.

Buying power – The dollar amount of securities that a client can purchase using only the (special memorandum) account balance and without depositing additional equity.

Call – An option contract giving the owner the right (not the obligation) to buy shares of stock at a strike price on or before the expiration date.

Call price – The price paid (usually a premium over the par value of the issue) for stocks or bonds redeemed prior to maturity of the issue.

Call spread – The result of an investor buying a call on a particular security and writing a call with a different expiration date, different exercise price or both on the same security.

Cash account – An account in which a client is required to pay in full for securities purchased by a specific date from the trade date.

Cover – 1) Futures purchased to offset a short position. 2) Being "long actuals" when shorting futures.

Covered call writer – An investor who writes a call and owns the stock or some other asset that guarantees the ability to perform if the call is exercised.

Cumulative MoneyStream™ – (also MoneyStream™ or CMS) A technical tool developed by Worden Brothers as a cumulative price/volume indicator. Upward sloping regression lines show patterns in buying and selling of stock.

Day order – A limit order with a specific duration of one day.

Fundamental Analysis (or fundamentals) – The study of a company's financial reports, marketing, management, and overall business characteristics as a means of determining the value of the stock (see technical analysis).

Hedge – A securities transaction that reduces the risk on an existing investment position.

In-the-money – A call option is said to be in-the-money if the current market value of the underlying interest is above the exercise price of the option. A put option is said to be in-the-money if the current market value of the underlying interest is below the exercise price of the option.

Initial margin requirement – The amount of equity a customer must deposit when making a new purchase in a margin account.

Initial Public Offering (IPO) – A company's initial public offering , sometimes referred to as "going public," is the first sale of stock by the company to the public.

Intrinsic value – The amount, if any, by which an option is in-the-money.

IRA – Individual Retirement Account; an account where contributions are tax deductible and gains are tax deferred.

LEAPS® – (Long-term Equity Anticipation Securities) An option with a long-term expiration date.

Long – Ownership of a stock or option; owning the security on which an option is written.

Long straddle – The act of buying a call and a put on a stock with the same strike price and expiration date.

Long-term Equity Anticipation Securities (LEAPS®) – An option with an extended expiration date, usually out one and two years and written in January of those years.

Margin – The amount of equity as a percentage of current market value in a margin account.

Margin account – An account in which a brokerage firm lends a client part of the purchase price of securities.

Margin call – A demand for a client to deposit money or securities when a purchase is made in excess of the value of a margin account, or if the collateral (margined securities) go down in value.

Market maker – A dealer willing to accept the risk of holding securities to facilitate trading in a particular security or securities.

Market order – An order to buy or sell a stock or option at the current market price.

Market value – The price at which an investor will buy or sell each share of common stock or each bond at a given time.

Married put – When an investor buys a stock and on the same day buys a put on a stock.

Monthly income preferred securities (MIPS) – Preferred stocks that pay monthly dividends.

Moving Average – An average that moves forward with time, dropping earlier components as later ones are added. This is an analytical tool which smooths out the fluctuations of a stock chart.

News driven – Any news about a security or stock that affects the volatility or the movement of that particular stock not by any intrinsic value to the company.

Option – The right to buy (or sell) a specified amount of a security (stocks, bonds, futures contracts, et cetera) at a specified price on or before a specific date (American style options).

Out-of-the-money – If the exercise price of a call (strike price) is above the current market value of the underlying interest, or if the exercise price of a put is below the current market value of the underlying interest, the option is said to be out of the money by that amount.

Over-the-counter (OTC) – A security that is not listed or traded on a major exchange.

Paper trade – A trade recorded and tracked, but not using actual funds in a brokerage account. These are done as a means of learning and testing a strategy (see *Simutrade*).

Price spread – A spread involving the purchase and sale of two options on the same stock with the same expiration date but with different exercise prices.

Put – An option contract that gives the owner the right to force the sale of a certain number of shares of stock at a specified price on or before a specific date.

Put spread – An investment in which an investor purchases one put on a particular stock and sells another put on the same stock but with a different expiration date, exercise price or both.

Range rider – A stock that has highs and lows on its price range and gradually rises to a high range over a period of time.

Resistance – The upper level of a stock's trading range at which a stock's price appears to be limited in upward movement (see *support*).

Reverse range rider – A stock that has highs and lows on its price range and gradually drops to a low range over a period of time.

Reverse stock split – An increase in the stock's par value by reducing the number of shares outstanding.

Rolling options – A strategy of buying calls or puts on a Rolling Stock.

Rolling Stock – A stock that fluctuates between a high and low price range for long periods of time and seems to be predictable due to the history of the stock.

Short – A condition resulting from selling an option or stock and not owning the particular securities.

Short hedge – A short securities or position protected by a long call position.

Short straddle – The position established by writing a call and a put on the same stock with the same strike price and expiration month.

Simutrade – A trade recorded and tracked, but not using actual funds in a brokerage account. These are done by traders as a means of learning and testing a strategy. (see *paper trade*).

Spread – 1) Consisting of being a buyer and seller of the same type of option with the options having different exercise prices and/or expiration dates. 2) The difference between the bid and the ask for a stock or option.

Stochastics – A technical indicator showing where the price of a stock is trading within a given range.

Stock split – A reduction in the par value of stock caused by the issuance of additional stock.

Stop limit order – A type of stop order which specifies the price at which the stock must trade.

Stop order – A limit order placed to protect account value from a significant decline in the price of a stock.

Straddle – Either a long or short position in a call and a put on the same security with the same expiration date and exercise price.

Strangle – A combination of a put and a call where both options are out-of-the-money. A strangle can be profitable only if the market is highly volatile and makes a major move in either direction.

Strike price – The price at which the underlying security will be sold if the option buyer exercises his/her rights in the contract.

Support – The lower level of a stock's trading range at which there appears to be a limit on further price declines.
(see *resistance*)

Technical Analysis (or technicals) – The study of stock charts, market sentiment, price, trading, and volume patterns to determine future price movements.
(see *fundamental analysis*)

Ticker symbol – A trading symbol used by a company to identify itself on a stock exchange.

Time Segmented Volume™ (TSV) – A proprietary technical indicator developed by Worden Brothers. TSV is an oscillator which is calculated by comparing various time segments of both price and volume.

Time value – Whatever the premium of the option is in addition to its intrinsic value.

Trendline – The long-term direction of a stock's movement as plotted on a chart.

Volatile – When speaking of the stock market and of stocks or securities, this is when the market or a particular stock's price tends to vary often and wildly.

INDEX I

REFERENCED COMPANIES

Name of Company (Ticker Symbol)

INDEX II
QUOTES BY AUTHOR

INDEX III

ROLLING STOCKS TOPICS